How To Answer...

"Do These Pants Make My Ass Look Fat?"

...And Get Laid Like Tile!

Athol Kay

Copyright © 2012 Athol Kay
All rights reserved.
ISBN: 1468158538
ISBN-13: 978-1468158533

Contents

Disclaimers

Acknowledgements

Introduction 1

1 - Down To Business 3

2 - A Little More On Alpha and Beta Male Traits 7

3 - Answering "Do These Pants Make My Ass Look Fat?" 11

4 - Dershowitz and Feinstein and the Legally Binding Threesome 14

5 - The Bridezilla Antidote: Those Bitches Are Just Hungry 20

6 - The Test 24

7 - Stray At Home Mom 27

8 - Beating Approach Anxiety – So Easy A Caveman Can Do It 31

9 - What To Do When Your Wife Won't Have Sex With You .. 35

10 - Dominance and Submission in Marriage: The Captain and First Officer Model 40

11 - The Dark Side Of Game 46

12 - Monogamy as a Sexual Strategy: My Wife Was Right All Along 50

13 - Oh Nice, Now My Wife Is Gaming Me Back 56

14 - Sexy Move: Biotone Advanced Therapy Massage Cream 58

15 - Don't Destroy Your Sex Rank By Stupid Educational Choices 59

16 - Sex During Pregnancy and Married Man Game 62

17 - Long Distance Relationship = Emotional Marathon 66

18 - Comfort Building Rituals 68

19 - Fitness Tests and My First Relationship Implosion 69

20 - What It Means When A Wife Says "I'm Bored." 71

21 - Fatherhood vs. Sexual Selection Failure 74

22 - I Love You But I'm Not In Love With You = Another Guy On The Radar 76

23 - Beware Of Asking For Marriage Advice From Close Friends 79

24 - Live Long And Prosper 82

25 - Sexy Move: Get Her To Cook You Breakfast 83

26 - If Women Are Naturally Submissive, Dominance Doesn't Need To Be Forced 85

27 - Foreign Women Make The Best Wives? 88

28 - Sexy Move: Rescue Her 91

29 - Male Mid-Life Crisis Is A Myth 92

30 - Female Mid-Life Crisis Is A Myth 94

31 - Only Boys Have Mojo 97

32 - Resistance Is Futile 98

33 - Samuel Adams: Not Always A Good Decision 100

34 - The Rhododendrons Of Unusual Size 102

35 - Sexy Move: Dirty Talk 105

36 - Sexy Move: Hit The Big Red Easy Button 106

37 - Sexy Move: Make The Bed Squeak 108

38 - Don't Move Out Just Because She Told You To 110

39 - Her Orgasm, Or Not Her Orgasm... What Was The Question? 113

40 - She's A Bad Bad Girl (Sometimes) 115

41 - The Second Date Rule 116

42 - Janet Loves Fred: How Much Fatter Does Janet Get? 117

43 - Say You're Sorry And Put It Right 118

44 - The Charity Event That Cannot Be Spoken Of 120

45 - Me So Hordey 122

46 - It's Not Your Job To Cure Their Sexual Dysfunction 123

47 - Understanding And Reacting To The Female Arm Slap . 125

48 - Jennifer Shuts Me Up 126

49 - Dad: 1945-2010 (A Letter Of Reference) 128

50 - Sexy Move: Disco Is Female Kryptonite 131

51 - Sexy Move: Find Some Stolen Time Together 133

52 - My Husband Is Scared Of Me 135

53 - If You Want A Personal Fuck Toy You Have To Be Willing To Be An Asshole 137

54 - The Splinter Of Mistrust And The Quest For 50 141

55 - Fried Tofu Explain Yourself 146

56 - Men Are Incapable Of Lying After Orgasm 148

57 - Don't Be A White Knight, Be A Horny Knight 150

58 - Don't Cater Endlessly To A SAHM 152

58 - Don't Cater Endlessly To A SAHM 152

59 - Sexy Move: Maybe She'd Love A Facial 154

60 - I Broke The Second Date Rule 156

61 - SAHM's Need To Be SAHM's "Plus Something." 160

62 - Christmas Tree Removal 101 166

63 - Play Blue's Clues Or Maybe You Lose 167

64 - The Propinquity Effect: A Third Wheel In Your Own Home Is You Being Stupid 169

65 - Sexy Move: Ask For Her Special Dish 172

66 - Sexting The Wife 174

67 - Life Sucks, The Marriage Still Good 176

68 - A Short Message From the Rationalization Hamster 178

69 - Cynical Advice on Responsible Non-Monogamy 180

70 - Be Playfully Mean To Girls Because They Like It 182

71 - How A Bad MMF Leads To Polyamory Weakly 184

72 - Jennifer Answers Some Questions 186

73 - The Highlight Reel Isn't Magic 189

74 - Female Hypergamy is Rational 196

75 - If She Offers You A Free Cookie – Take The Cookie 197

76 - The Red Pill, The Nookie and The Best Revenge 201

77 - Temptation 203

78 - Her Needs For Stimulation And Relationship Engagement 204

79 - Girl Game: Have Long Hair 208

80 - Girl Game: Find Out What Turns Him On 210

81 - Girl Game: Initiate Sex By Touching Him On The Penis .. 213

82 - Girl Game: Give Him A Fair Warning 215

83 - The Third Wheel 217

84 - Jennifer and the Two Hundred Pound Raccoon 220

85 - Girl Game: Post-Coital Cuddling 222

86 - Living With A Big Cat 224

87 - Taken In Hand vs. Captain and First Officer 228

88 - Don't Wait.. 231

89 - How To Purposely Fall Out Of Love As Quickly As Possible 234

90 - Sometimes It All Gets To Me.................................. 238

91 - Why Men Are So Paranoid About Girls Night Out........ 240

92 - Forgive And Move On Together.............................. 242

93 - How To Build Self-Esteem...................................... 244

94 - It's Big, It's White And She Can't Wait To Get Her Hands On It.. 245

95 - Functional, Productive and Happy.............................. 249

96 - Shit My Husband Says: Ocean Voyage...................... 252

97 - The Main Complaint About Monogamy Is That It Works 254

98 - The Best Pussy I Ever Had...................................... 257

99 - Sexting and Jennifer's Lost Phone............................. 261

100 - Due Diligence Before You Marry............................. 264

101 - The Sci-fi Thing And Just Being Yourself...................... 267

Further Resources 271

About the Author and his Wife... 272

Disclaimers

I am not a marriage counselor. I did look into becoming one a while back but discovered I would need two years formal study and the starting money was around $33,000 a year. I figured Jennifer would divorce me if I made that little.

This book is not intended to replace the advice and instruction of your own medical, legal or marriage or other licensed providers. It's certainly not meant to replace advice from plumbers or electricians either. If something requires licensed professionals, use them and follow their advice.

In real life I am a nurse. However I am not your nurse, nor am I providing any form of nursing service to any reader.

Readers hold me harmless for negative outcomes based on following any suggestions on this book. Every relationship is different, not everything will work.

Sex is a very primal need. Sometimes the book touches on the darker aspects of human nature. Understanding and discussing these darker elements within us all, is not the same as advocating for them.

Acknowledgments

Some of the ideas in this book are new, but the greater part of them has been based on the work of countless others. Some notables:

The Talk About Marriage forum, The "Manosphere", Dr. Helen Fisher, "Mystery", Roissy, Evolutionary Psychology and being in the field of Nursing

Many people have helped me along the way with my work. Some notables:

Marcus Doran Consulting have been of enormous support with the upgrading of my website and marketing insight.

Heather Yuhas worked tirelessly on the cover.

Cynthia Lang Photography managed to make Mr. Potatohead look more like Steve Jobs. Quite amazing.

My endless thanks to Mum, Dad and of course my wife Jennifer.

My apologies to my teenage daughters for being the embarrassing father writing about sex. In time I hope it stops being embarrassing and is just a little awkward and weird.

One of the things that has been exceedingly humbling over the last two years is that I have gained a readership that cares about spreading the word for what I do. I have fans. I truly hope that what I write has helped you all, for you have all helped me.
.

Introduction

This is a book about sex and marriage, but it's not a very typical one. Let me explain in a roundabout way...

My family quite likes Chinese food for dinner and we order it fairly frequently. I love Chinese pork spare ribs, Jennifer loves the vegetables in sauce, my eldest daughter loves fried rice, and my youngest daughter is crazy for dumplings. So we all get what we want to eat and are happy. But we can never eat it all, and we always have lots leftover.

So the next day we slice up all the leftover dumplings, spring rolls, ribs or whatever we have, and throw all the leftovers in a fry pan with a little oil. Because it's all Chinese food, it all just works together so well... the result is the most amazing stir fry dish you'll ever have. It's a little taste of everything, "Every mouthful an adventure." ™

My first book *The Married Man Sex Life Primer 2011* (aka "the Primer") was a solid textbook for married guys looking to improve their sex lives and marriage. I kept it as light as I could, but ultimately it's a big structured organized book that I had to rewrite over and over. At first I was worried that I didn't have enough content to get that book to 200 pages, in the end it finished at 344 pages and it could have easily been bigger.

When I said it could easily have been bigger, my first book ran 120,000 words long, but through 2010-2011, I've written around 400,000 words on my blog Married Man Sex Life. So I have about 280,000 words of leftovers that never made it into the first book. And to be honest, some of the stuff that didn't make it into my first book is my best and most popular writing, but it just didn't fit in.

So this book is my second book, and it's my "Chinese leftovers stir-fry" book. It's the stuff that was just too off topic for the Primer. The stories that were funny as hell, but slowed the Primer down. The posts that were really just more personal in nature. There are some serious pieces as well and there are some sharp jabbing ones too.

Also I find that I have to physically be in the act of writing, to do my best thinking. So there are also some posts included that are to me "historically important" in that as I have written them, I've had my best ideas and thoughts.

A couple of definitions are in order as well. "Sex Rank" refers to the age old 1-10 scale of hotness. "Body Agenda" refers to the way our bodies seek to strategize ways to create children subconsciously. "PUA" stands for Pickup Artist. You'll hit a post defining Alpha and Beta in the second chapter so that can wait for now.

So anyway, grab a seat at the table. You're going to love this stuff.

1 - Down To Business

January 2, 2010

Hi there and welcome to Married Man Sex Life.

My name is Athol and I'm 39 years old headed towards the big 40. I've been married for 15 years and Jennifer and I have two daughters together age 10 and 12. Our life together is pleasantly uncomplicated, and we're mercifully free of the drama of step-families, baby's daddy's, divorce and affairs. We've had our share of tricky pregnancies, cancer scares and dental bills. Life is pretty normal; I'm just not saying we're living a charmed life beyond all reason. It's a life together, not a TV show. My marriage is by no means perfect. I'm not perfect, Jennifer isn't perfect, but we're doing much better than most.

Anyway here's the thing, I've never been overly excited about the idea of marriage. Don't get me wrong, I've always been crazy about Jennifer. I mean three years long distance before we married crazy. I'm talking leave your country of origin crazy. She always seemed to like the idea, and honestly I never really thought about what I was doing getting married. I just wanted to sleep with her. All. The. Time. So I just got married to her. No question of whether it was really a good idea or not.

The first year was exciting. As in I'm finally having sex happy, but also with a couple of freak out "wow this really has to work because I'll be deported and I'm risking everything" crazy moments. As it turned out we just clicked. No real major conflicts, just building a life together. We've worked together at the same job for most of our marriage. House, kids, medical insurance, the whole deal.

So fast forward...

We're hitting 15 years together, and apparently that's twice the national average. People are saying that it's impressive like we've discovered cold fusion or something. But like I said earlier, I wasn't really that excited by marriage. It wasn't a real problem to me that needed solving, so I wasn't really bothered by it. I was still getting laid like tile by Jennifer as well. So all good on that front.

Then one of my clients... that's one of my special needs kids at work, corners me into a one sided conversation telling me over and over "I know all about you, you've got that ring on your finger, you're the married man." And he said the words "Married Man" the same way doctors pronounce someone dead. The same way a two year old announces someone is fat. Like it was some sort of final definition that couldn't be argued with. Pretty soon that whole work area just started calling me "Married Man", like my superhero secret identity had suddenly been spilled.

So here's the thing. I was in the middle of what amounted to a little bit of a mid life crisis. Wondering about a few of my choices, and the consequences of them. Wondering in particular if my marriage is one of the better ones. Because as I said earlier, I never really thought about marriage before, just ploughed ahead into the whole deal. But I can hardly think clearly because I'm getting mind control top up sex most every night from Jennifer. The Jezebel!

So there I was in the middle of wondering if marriage was even something I was interested in... and I have medically diagnosable developmentally disabled people calling me "The Married Man."

And then it hits me...

What if my marriage was in fact the defining aspect of my entire life? What if I was actually really good at being married, you know the same way say Tiger Woods is good at golf. Oh... perhaps he's a bad example just now, but you get my drift. So I'd discovered I was actually pretty good at marriage, and like I say, Jennifer I'm still crazy about. But I didn't really know why I was good at marriage. So I went looking to find out....

Somewhere between ex-girlfriends, my first fiancé that could have been that I passed on, my sociology degree, international travel, being a male nurse for 14 years and surrounded by women and listening to them complain about husbands and boyfriends, the hundreds to maybe a thousand books I've read over the years around sexuality, relationships, biology, psychology and so on I'm finally coming to a point where I'm understanding the why of why I'm good. I passed on working towards a Masters Degree in Marriage Counseling because I Googled to find out how much those guys make. (I thought my wife might divorce me if I only made $33,000 a year as a starting point. Sorry, but $33,000 for a Masters LOL.) The great news is that most of the "why" isn't even that hard to do.

What I've done, I've done to this point mainly for my own interest. Like I keep saying, I was never mentally excited about marriage. Now I realize it's as vital to me as the air I breathe. As important to me as... oh... *my relationship to Jennifer!*

One of the places I'd discovered in my travels was an Internet forum called *Talk About Marriage*. I'd read posts there over and over and at times be reduced to fits of laughter or cringe in horror at some of the things going down in other people's lives or things people just let happen to them. About once a day I just can't believe what I'm reading and walk over to Jennifer and deep kiss her in relief. Mid-life crisis FIXED. I posted advice and mostly it's well received. I still post over there. I'd started getting a lot of private messages and thanks for my advice. But I had to repeat myself for too many new people there, and frankly by the time they had reached the Talk About Marriage board things often just seemed too late to do anything. So I've decided that I just need a bigger platform to speak from.

Primarily I'm speaking to men. Women are always welcome of course and you will get value from this, I'm by no means anti-women, but what I have to say, I have to say primarily for men. Mostly what I expect is a lot of women will find this blog first and beg their husbands to read it. If the reason you are reading here is your wife asked / told / demanded you did – take that as a serious wake up call.

My approach to marriage is part a married spin on Pickup Artist "Game", part Evolutionary Psychology, part Sex Ed, and part Self-Help. Mostly it's about learning what it is about you that unlocks the Holy Grail between your wife's legs. I will caution you though, some of this stuff I have to tell you is not going to be easy to read. It's the Red Pill for those that dare.

So anyway…. you're here for a reason. I think I have some of the answers you may need. So if you want to pull up a chair, I'll tell you what I know.

2 - A Little More On Alpha and Beta Male Traits

January 21, 2010

Most discussions of Alpha and Beta Males see the relationship between them to be polar opposites. In other words, you are either an Alpha Male, or a Beta Male, with not much in between the two. Occasionally you get a reference to an Omega Male who is so terrible at everything that he falls below even the lowest of Betas.

The ranking system has Alpha Males at the top of the ladder, and they typically have lots of sex partners and/or shorter term relationships. In the middle are the Beta Males, who typically try and have one consistent long term partner. Below that comes the Omega Males, who just can't get laid.

However as I've said before, I see Alpha Male and Beta Male, as not simply a fixed status, but as a collection of traits. Having nothing but only one set of either traits, nets you the stereotypical "Aipha Male" or "Beta Male." In truth most of us have some Alpha and some Beta in us, but it's not a zero sum game.

The Alpha Traits are the more traditional and physically based traits. Size, strength, fitness, aggression, violence, dominance, beauty, health, confidence, fearlessness, daring, hand eye co-ordination, speed etc are all skills and abilities that are simply excellent for survival as a small tribal group on the ancient savannah. Display of these skills generates a seemingly hardwired sexual attraction response in women. On some level we are still approaching sex wired exactly the same as we were 10,000+ years ago.

The Beta Traits are the more modern and socially based traits. Size and strength matter less and less in the modern age. Skill with paperwork is the key to income in most fields. Violence is no longer a tool for social advancement, but results in becoming a social outcast or jailed. What matters in the modern age is the ability to stay calm, sociable, nice, patient, verbal, kind, clever, cuddly, soothing, diplomatic, kid friendly and emotionally available. It's ideal for working in cubicles and service industries. This is what women need from a modern partner to establish a working relationship to create a home and have an income in order to raise children. Without this support, women become deeply uncomfortable and this can short circuit sexual desire.

As you can see, the Alpha Traits and the Beta Traits are worlds apart. But as I say, these are not opposite skill sets. The true format is this:

High Alpha, Low Beta = "Alpha Male" "Bad Boy"

Low Alpha, High Beta = "Beta Male" "Nice Guy"

Low Alpha, Low Beta = "Omega Male" "Total Loser"

High Alpha, High Beta = "Gamma Male" "Married Game"

The Omega Male is easiest to dispense with. He's just devoid of positive qualities and only the most desperate of women would desire to mate with him. Even then he'll likely end up being supported by her to some degree. Avoid him.

The pure Alpha Bad Boys certainly do pull the women, but the relationships tend to be short as eventually the women become uncomfortable with the lack of comfort building support. There's plenty of excitement, and sizzling sex as the attraction is definitely there for her, but she knows from the beginning it's not going to last, but she is drawn to him anyway.

The pure Beta Nice Guys also pull women, but they pull differently. They "make sense" on an intellectual level and they are very comfortable to live with. More than likely they are too comfortable, and the woman tends to want to see a display of dominance of some sort before she becomes fully attracted to him. Ultimately the Nice Guys are just too sexually boring to women to remain completely focused on one. Cue up the "I love you, but I'm not in love with you speech."

What is often seen in young women is ping ponging between Bad Boys and Nice Guys – she gets a dose of crazy sexual attraction from the Bad Boy, but then she needs the comfort building and she seeks it from a Nice Guy, and then the cycle repeats over and over until the music stops around age thirty-five and she's scrambling to find a chair anywhere.

The ideal is the Gamma Male. They are not often talked about, but they are out there. Usually a Gamma is an Alpha Male that "grew up" and toned down the antics slightly and started being socially conscious and more of a team player. Or they started as a Beta Male that "grew a pair" and started bumping back on the rest of the world rather than just taking it lying down. Either way works as a route. Like Jean-Luc Picard, Gammas use diplomacy but when required to they will respond with adept force. Mostly they are consciously aware of both their own natures, and the needs of women. They adjust on the fly to the situation, sometimes hard, sometimes soft.

Gamma's are the true ideal, but I think the Alpha and Beta terms are so ingrained, that it is simply easier to broken record the idea that if you're too Alpha the solution is to add Beta, and if you're too Beta the solution is to add Alpha.

You already know what your weak area is. Work on that for easy gains.

Picard didn't get laid very much on the shows... but are you telling me he couldn't if he wanted to?

3 - Answering "Do These Pants Make My Ass Look Fat?"

January 30, 2010

There comes a time in every man's life, when the woman he is involved with asks the dreaded question.

"Do these pants make my ass look fat?" (DTPMMALF)

Guys tend to be simple creatures with basic needs. Feed us, let us have a place to sleep and some form of entertainment and we usually run at 95% of maximum happiness. Most guys will automatically attempt to answer any question with a one word answer. Unfortunately the only words that spring to mind are either "yes" or "no."

Answering "yes" is of course a terrible choice. If you can't figure out why on your own, you're probably not salvageable as a male. (Also those kids calling you Dad probably aren't yours either – just a heads up)

Answering "no" is not the relationship suicide that answering "yes" is, but if you watch her face carefully you will not see any enjoyment in hearing a "no" answer. "No" is not the right answer, somehow you have failed.

Occasionally someone will attempt to answer DTPMMALF by neither answering "yes" nor "no" and advancing a cautious "maybe" as an answer. The Maybe Gambit does work as an answer, but – and this is important – it works only if you are her girlfriend or a gay friend.

You answering "maybe" just makes you seem completely developmentally delayed. You are expected to have strong well formed opinions on the state of her body. Have you been paying attention to her at all?

The other attempted answer is the It's All In Your Head Defense where you explain that she is somehow mentally unstable for asking the question. This is the best of the answers so far, but is essentially an insult at heart and drives the two of you a little further apart. Don't use it.

The Actual Question Being Asked

Having covered what not to answer DTPMMALF with, it's time to find out what to answer DTPMMALF with. Let's break down DTPMMALF into something simple enough for the average guy to understand. When she says,

"Do these pants make my ass look fat?"

You should hear,

"Xx xxxxx xxxxx xxxx xx ass xxxx xxx?"

Removing the verbal clutter, it is summarized to,

"ass?"

The correct response to that question is your first and natural response. I.e. "yes of course I'd like some ass." Remember how the "no" answer didn't please her? See how you screwed that up now?

So how do you answer DTPMMALF - and get laid.

Give her your best I'm-a-sly-dog-naughty-boy smile. Hold the smile and make eye contact for at least 3–5 seconds until she stops whatever she is doing and pays complete attention to you. Then say…

"I don't know. I would have to see your ass without the pants."

Then just wait expectantly, continuing to hold eye contact.

Now What Happens?!?!

One of two things will happen. Either she takes the pants off or she doesn't. If she takes them off... close the deal. If she doesn't take them off she should have at least smiled letting you know you answered the question correctly. That means good things will happen to you from her in the near future. Don't be a twit and blow it.

Warning About Answering DTPMMALF Correctly.

Women only ask this question when they are in the fertile part of their monthly cycle.

4 - Dershowitz and Feinstein and the Legally Binding Threesome

February 14, 2010

(Edit: "John" and "Jodi" refer to the first names of the prior and then current Connecticut governors.)

As I said in my very first post, I've never been particularly excited about marriage. I've certainly been very excited about my wife, most notably in the tearing her underwear off and holding her down department. Marriage was just kind of a hoop to jump through on the way to the bedroom. Like the church was a location bounce for a compliance test. I just plowed ahead and completed all the tasks required. Propose check. Ring check. Wedding check. Booty on tap check. *Alright.*

It wasn't until much later that I discovered I liked being married, and realized I liked the idea of marriage. Last year was the long difficult 14th year of marriage where I did an enormous amount of reading and thinking about marriage. Deciding and discovering I was in fact pro-marriage (if only for myself) was a surprise to me. However one of the greatest shocks to me last year was the discovery that someone else had been sneaking into our bed for the entire time we have been married.

John had been sneaking in for the first nine years of our marriage. If that wasn't bad enough, when the thing with John ended, the bed didn't even have time to get cold before Jodi slipped in and she took up residence. And that's been going on for nearly six years.

Both my wife and I were appalled. All we wanted was each other and somehow it had turned into a threesome. Naturally we called Dershowitz and Feinstein (as an aside that phrase "Dershowitz and Feinstein" doubles as my wife's safe word for episodes of underwear tearing and holding her down. It gets a better response than the old one of "the children!" because I'd frequently mistake it as her asking to switch it up into make a baby style pounding and there were some disagreements about what she meant) and... hang on, long parenthesis... Naturally we called Dershowitz and Feinstein and asked them for help. Is there any way we can get Jodi out of our lives and bed?

Turns out there isn't. We can kick Jodi out at any time, but apparently the fine print says if we want her out, we have to divorce. Jodi and Co apparently wrote the fine print on the marriage law, and like fools when we did the whole church thing we signed a marriage license. I don't even remember signing the license, the whole day is fuzzy with booze, getting the photos done and having every female member of her extended family touch my ass on the dance floor. Anyway, we signed and boom, John moved in. Nine years later he moved out, and gave his set of keys to Jodi and she moved in. Awesome... more tea Jodi? Make yourself at home.

So anyway Jodi basically leaves us alone, which is good, except anytime we have some sort of discussion about being married or the wedding. Then she's always sticking her nose in. Let me give you an example... my wife and I firmly believe that marriage is meant to last forever, we said that in the church for the wedding vows. I could prove that by going to the video of the wedding, but it's on a VHS, accidentally taped over with a really good episode of Teletubbies from when the kids were little, and purposely lost.

Anyway... we agreed that marriage was forever, no matter what. We made vows. Sweet precious vows. In sickness and in health, for richer for poorer, for World of Warcraft addiction and Irritable Bowel Syndrome. For love and uncontrollable flatulence.

Jodi always kind of rolls her eyes a little at that. She just says that Connecticut is a No Fault divorce state, and basically anytime either one of us wants out she'll be happy to tear up the marriage license and start deciding how to divide up half of everything. When we tell her "we made vows, though", she just sips her tea and says it's all a verbal agreement and inadmissible in a court of law.

"In fact" she says, "you could have said nothing in that little church, or you could have said vows in Latin, Elvis could have been your best man, Joan of Arc the Maid of Honor and Moses could have done the service and it all wouldn't matter any different."

She paused for effect... "You could have just sung Puff the Magic Dragon to each other for all I care. The marriage license is your consent to the marriage agreement as defined by Connecticut Marriage Law. That's what your marriage agreement is."

We look across at Dershowtiz and Feinstein. They look bored.

I chime in with a question, "so what is our marriage actually an agreement for?"

Jodi looks over her glasses, "well getting married allows you to enjoy all the rights, benefits and responsibilities of marriage."

"So what are the rights, benefits and responsibilities of marriage?" I ask.

"Well I'm afraid that's not actually defined in Connecticut Law."

"That seems a bit of a lapse doesn't it? That just leaves it as a license to do something."

"Well we'd prefer to not actually meddle in private affairs of the people if we could. It's really all just for figuring out taxes to be honest."

"It's all just about tax filing?!?!?"

Jodi looks disapprovingly at me in a tight frown, "you're not very romantic are you Mr. Kay. It's what you make of it; I would have thought you would have figured that out by now."

"Ok, I have to ask then. Sex. What about sex then?"

"I'm just a metaphor for the State of Connecticut, you can't have sex with me, it's not possible." Jodi looked over at Jennifer for a moment and gently patted her on the arm, "I see what you mean dear, he's like this all the time isn't he."

"No, I mean I've only had sex with one person for the last 15 years because that's the agreement. That's in the law right? One of the rights, benefits and responsibilities of marriage is sex right?"

"Oh no, we took the adultery laws off the books long ago. Frightfully messy things to police really. Waste of tax money trying to control all that."

"What? You mean there's no sexual agreement to marriage? To be faithful?"

"You're awfully old fashioned aren't you? No, no there's no sexual aspect defined in marriage law. Anyone can have sex with whoever they want in Connecticut as long as they are of the age of consent and all that sort of thing. You can have lots of sex, some sex, no sex, sex with anyone inside or outside your marriage; it's not really relevant to me. As I've told you before, marriage is really all about the tax. And I can break up that tax arrangement any time either one of you want."

Jodi helped herself to a shortbread cookie. Dunked once and bit off a small piece. "Listen, I don't really like to meddle, but just this once I'll give some advice," another dunk and another bite, "as I said before marriage is what you make of it, and as you know it can stop at any moment if one of you wants out."

Then she crushed the rest of the shortbread cookie in her fist and dropped the crumbles into the tea cup. The she very slowly and pointedly tipped the cup over on the table and let it spill a slow spreading puddle across the cloth.

"Pay attention to each other. Don't get sloppy. No one likes cleaning up someone else's mess." Then she sat back into the sofa with finger raised as if to say something more, but she closed her eyes mid thought and her hand eased down to her lap.

Then it hit me. "Holy crap I can have sex with anyone I want!" Holy crap I might have said that out loud.

Jennifer is a listener more than a talker and she had been silent for the whole conversation. With Jodi sleeping, Jen held me close for a few seconds. I'm tall and she is short, so she pulled me down to her and softly whispered in my ear...

"Dershowitz and Feinstein."

And two spring loaded briefcases popped open across the table, ready for action...

"We can do that if you want," I said softly as I delicately found a good handhold of brunette hair and tugged gently. "You'd still want to fuck me after the divorce."

Then I kissed her...

... and led her upstairs to explain things... in greater detail.

Getting married is not a permanent finishing line to sexual competition. Sex ranking issues continue into the marriage, and a consistent DHV (Display of High Value) is an ongoing requirement.

No Connecticut governors were harmed in the making of this post. I have no idea if Jodi Rell likes either tea or shortbread cookies, or falls asleep mid sentence. It's a metaphor.

5 - The Bridezilla Antidote: Those Bitches Are Just Hungry

February 16, 2010

One of the most basic attraction triggers hard wired into us from The Time Before Writing is bringing a member of the opposite sex food. Women have long known this and the old line is that the way to a man's heart is through his stomach. It's really no different for women, that's what the whole taking them out to dinner thing is about. Yeah taking them out to dinner is really just the modern version of bringing the tribe a dead gazelle and handing out meat. Throg good hunter. We mate now. (You know some cave-girls were thinking to themselves "Shit… which part of a gazelle equals a handjob?")

Now imagine what actually knowing how to cook food does to your Sex Rank… you can provide food… not only will you not starve if left alone, but women very much respond to men capable of cooking. I'm not saying you get married and turn into Iron Chef, but pulling some of the cooking duties in the home is a huge plus. It's a life skill, and any display of skill is a display of higher value.

Now to actually push mere cooking into "Food Game", you're going to need some absolutely "OMFG WHO MADE THIS?!" reaction inducing recipes.

Today we're doing bread pudding. I spent literally 4-5 years making this about once every 3-4 weeks until I got the recipe perfect. The last 10 years it's been unchanged. I can absolutely assure you that I have pulled rooms of women with this recipe. Once you have this recipe down you have one of the most potent pieces of dessert known to man. Women – as in "all" women love bread pudding. It's warm, it's sweet (but not too sweet), it's soft and rich, it smells great and the first bite is as good as the last. Not everyone has tried bread pudding, but one spoonful nets a convert. It's like that scene in the second Matrix movie where the French guy has that specially coded piece of chocolate cake and the blond in the red dress eats it and has to run to the bathroom orgasming. It's probably best to... go check on her...

So... have your attention yet?

You will need.

1 Stick of Butter
3 Cups of Milk (not fat free!)
1 Cup Brown Sugar
3 Eggs
1 Tsp of Cinnamon
2 Shots of Kahlua
1 loaf of cinnamon raisin bread

Step 1 - Turn the oven on to 350 F. If you can't manage this step, ask your group home staff for assistance. They are here to help and they love you.

Step 2 - Put the three cups of milk into a pot and place on a fairly low heat. Chop up the butter into smallish chunks and add to the milk. The idea here is just to melt the butter into the milk making a buttery milky mix. Don't boil the milk or anything daft, just melt the butter into the mildly warm milk as you do the rest of the steps.

Step 3 - Mix the eggs, brown sugar, cinnamon and Kahlua together in a big bowl. A teaspoon of cinnamon is by man measurement "a really big sprinkle." Two shots of Kahlua is really just one shot by Mark I Eyeball that screwed up into a "whoops a bit much." You will end up with a dark brown gooey slime.

Step 4 - Chop up the cinnamon raisin bread. I cut each slice into about 16 pieces. So that's three cuts one way, then turn the bread and three cuts the other. Manly men usually just do four slices at a time and show off their knife skills to the ladies. So four slices at a time would make 64 little tiny cubes of cinnamon raisin bread. Which isn't important to anyone but engineers, but I like to please everyone...

Step 5 - Seeing the average loaf of cinnamon raisin bread has 18 slices, add exactly 288 small cubes of cinnamon raisin bread to the dark brown gooey slime created in Step 3. Now using a spatula (not your hands... the use of tools is the original Alpha Male skill, gentlemen) mix the bread and the goop together until the whole thing is evenly spread all over the bread. It's a kind of dig down to the bottom of the bowl and roll motion. This is why a big bowl was important.

Step 6 - By now the butter should be pretty melted into the milk. Pour about 2.5 cups worth of the milk over the bread and goop. Once the bread looks like it has soaked up the milk a bit, transfer the whole thing into a good sized casserole dish and use the spatula to even it out. You can add a little more milk to the casserole dish if you like. I find the best ratio is keep adding milk, but not so much that you see puddles forming on the surface.

Step 7 - Bake at 350 F for 1 hour uncovered.

And that's it. Let it cool off a bit. Start making friends. This is a perfect and I mean perfect big family gathering dessert. You can make it the day before and it's even better the second day. I get mad Preselection props as the women drool over this and me. My wife is like "three drinks agreeable" after a serving of this. It's 10-15 minutes prep time to make, 1 hour to bake. So easy, so good. Make it good once and your wife will beg for it forever. Bring it out a few times a year. Relish the adoration.

Warning: Bread Pudding May Cause Ovulation.

I did make a batch last night to take photos of for this post. Kids are off school this week and a gaggle of friends were invited over while I was at work. Apparently it's a huge hit with 5th and 7th grade girls as well. I'll update next time I make it. Once the spatula is out of the dishwasher I'm going after the ringleader....

6 - The Test

February 20, 2010

Imagine you're a humble 6 married to a 7 and the sex life is mediocre at best. Then you stumble onto Married Man Sex Life and discover the basic principles I cover and put them into action.

You work out, are nicer at home, earn a little more money, dress better, play with the kids and so on. When you go from a 6 to a 7 everything is great and the sex life gets better. So you keep plowing ahead and continue to develop yourself further. When you hit Sex Rank 8, the sex at home starts getting really good. You wife loves the new you and can't help but respond to you.

Then comes the test. Failing this test will probably undo everything you've done to improve things with your wife in one easy move.

Here's how it plays out. You sister-in-law, your wife's best friend, your female work friend, the chick behind the counter at Starbucks, one of the Mom's at your kids school... say she's a 6 or a 7. See before when you were a 6, you were off the market and she wasn't interested in you. Pulling you off your wife would have taken a lot of effort, and let's face it, you were just a 6.

But now... now you're an 8, that's a whole different deal. She's interested in you. She can't help it as attraction isn't a choice. She may not even be consciously aware of it, but you are far more interesting to her sexually now. Women throw off dozens of small signals of sexual interest that the alert man can notice...

Hair flipping and stroking.
Reapplying lipstick.
Licking lips.
Smiling.
Eye contact.
Touching her body, specially her neck area.
Dressing better when she expects to see you.
Sitting with her body orientated towards yours.
Sitting with legs open towards you.
Laughing easily at your jokes – even if they are not particularly good.
Taking an article of clothing off in front of you.
Small acts of service that aren't required.
Seeking to stand or sit near you.
Increased breathing rate.
Eager to see you.
Unnecessary phone calls, emails, text messages just to create contact with you.
Touching you in any way.

So what's going to happen is that one day you're going to be having a great conversation with a woman, not even trying to consciously run Game on her... and you'll just suddenly realize that she's doing half the things on the list above. Then you realize it's just a case of turning up the heat a little, being a little more forward and she will probably sleep with you eventually. Just instigate, isolate, and escalate. Keep it discreet and she will fall.

Discreet is interesting and quite key to seduction. I once answered a phone call as a female friend was laughing at one of my jokes. In my response to the question "And who are you with?" by the caller, I replied "Oh I don't kiss and tell." Just that phrase alone turned her positively crimson and then she completely took down her hair, shook it out and refixed it, then removed her scarf and just hung out with me longer than she needed to. I see what you did there.

The point is, it's not going to be some super hot 10 dressed in fishnets and not much else wanting to get back at her boyfriend that's going to be your test. Megan Fox won't be your test. It's going to be someone close to you, someone you probably have known for a while, even feel friendly and emotionally connected to that is going to be your test. You may not see coming until it's close to the point of no return.

And you will absolutely love every second of it while in proximity to this woman. You're programmed to like it.

The great difficulty of temptation, is that it's... tempting. No matter how wonderful sex at home is, new pussy is incredibly tasty. Once you can read a woman's indicators of interest, and you know the basics of seduction, having a little piece of something on the side becomes not just a fantasy, but an easy possibility. Emotions can run high. You may be more hooked in to the other woman than you know. At least while you're standing next to her anyway.

And all this is going to be happening just as everything you've worked for with your wife responding to you coming together. And if your wife is even halfway paying attention to you, she'll know something is up.

So while I'm not telling you what is right and what is wrong, be aware of the long term risks for a little fun. Wives hate being cheated on. The damage you do will likely be permanent.

7 - Stray At Home Mom

February 21, 2010

Ah the Stay At Home Mother. Rosy cheeked children in clean clothes. Happy husband greeted at the door with a fresh application of lipstick and the smell of dinner. I admit it, I want that, sounds wonderful. But just like a Disney vacation, for most of us it's just a pleasant fantasy experience rather than something you can actually afford.

Back in the 1950s it was possible for a regular guy to hold a job that could support a family alone, and there was enough physical labor in the home to require a "full time employee" doing the stuff in the house. As women entered the workforce in greater and greater numbers, it actually flooded the labor market with an oversupply of labor and devalued the average worker's paycheck. Loosely speaking, the same sort of job in 1950 that would have supported a family, supports about half a family today. So back in the 1960s and 1970s and even 1980s, a woman entering the workforce was all about "choice for women", but by 2010 there is no real choice for women anymore and if they don't get a freaking job and work it the same way a man has to, the family will go bankrupt. Plus with modern appliances, housework is vastly easier these days than in 1950, and there are typically less children to care for as well. So there is far less need to have a wife solely "work at home."

Understand that I'm not saying this is right or wrong, I'm just telling you what happened. And just to be clear, I see the pre-1950s housewife as having a serious workload, nowadays though, not so much. In fact I doubt most modern SAHMs even have half the skill set or work ethic of a 1950s SAHM. Ask yourself which one could probably make clothes and which one can't sew a button. Guess which one can get a quick meal on the table in a time crunch with creative use of leftovers, and which one dials for a pizza.

Now I certainly agree that many SAHM are doing a fine job of house and child care and holding up their end of the agreement of helping propel a husband to fame, glory and a higher paycheck. If you want to pop out a small army of children, a SAHM (or SAHD) is quite probably cost effective. However I suspect for many women today the SAHM lifestyle is a pipedream of what amounts to early retirement at the expense of their husband who must work insane hours outside the home.

Furthermore, there is not enough actual work to do in the home, especially with only one or two pre-school children. Which leaves the SAHM with far too much free time and boredom, and free time and boredom is the seed and soil for a woman to seek an affair. There's nothing quite like getting rewarded for pulling extra shifts, by your wife chatting on Facebook with an old boyfriend and her complaining to him that she's lonely because you're always working. Sure here's a photo of my tits, but I shouldn't really be doing this. I just put the baby down for a nap, so I have about an hour and a half. (If she's on MySpace she is definitely cheating on you.)

If a two income family wife is lazy, stupid and careless at her job, she will risk getting fired and there are immediate consequences for that. So it tends to be self correcting in that the wife will attempt to adjust her work performance to ensure she is not fired. Outside forces will ensure she continues to pull her weight for the family.

If a SAHM is lazy, stupid and careless at her job... the husband isn't truly her employer, and termination for lack of job performance is basically divorce. This is an appalling option to have to choose. Furthermore thanks to alimony, the husband will have to continue to "pay her" for the job she wasn't doing during the marriage after the divorce is final. So there is a serious moral hazard for the wife in that she can continue to fail at her job of SAHM and still get paid. Or as one of my readers in the middle of divorcing his Stray At Home wife puts it, "She says she doesn't need a husband, just my money." Simply awesome.

Now whether a couple decides to go the two income family route, or worker drone and SAHM route, is completely up to them. I just think for a modern husband you have to evaluate very carefully the character and work ethic of your wife when she floats the idea of her being a SAHM. (Really this is something to talk about and evaluate before you marry, but the little head is usually in charge around the getting married time so it's understandable how mistakes can be made) If you don't see a bunch of Suzy Q homemaker stuff going on now, you won't see a bunch of that stuff magically happening after she turns into a SAHM. I'm talking about meals from scratch, baking, decorating, house cleaning skill, an obvious love of children and joyous babysitting for friends with kids yada yada yada. Knitting... show me your knitting sweetheart. Can you even do a scarf?

Put another way... if you were an employer and interviewing women for the position of SAHM, does she show any of the skills the job requires? If she doesn't, pass on her as a wife, or simply state she gets a job like everybody else. Welcome to life in the 21st Century. Thank feminism and birth control pills, men had nothing to do with this.

The other thing to watch for is the easy way women can just extend their SAHM contract for another five to six years at will. You forgot your pills huh..... You just forgot them. Really. This has never happened before in all of human history. Alert the news media. You just forgot. That's just super. Really, really super. No I'm so excited about the new addition to the family. Can't wait. Just super, super excited. Tears of happiness darling, tears of happiness.

No doubt I'm going to catch flak by saying there's not enough work to do in the home for a SAHM to actually do. In my defense, when my two kids where little I was the SAHD... plus I held down a full time nursing job during the nights and weekends. I can very much assure you that my time at home with my own children was far easier than my time on the job dealing with the total care of developmentally disabled adults. The difference between diapering or feeding a cranky toddler and a combative wheelchair bound adult is quite significant.

As a final thought – for many couples the cost of child care is pretty extreme for pre-school kids. Having one parent home during the week and still doing something part time makes a lot of sense financially. However once you hear that spending time with just one or two children is just so exhausting that the extra job just isn't possible, you're looking down the barrel of the Mother of All Fitness Tests. You'll be told that it's not about her needs; it's for the children, the children the children the children. Your reply to that is that the family needs a certain level of income, and they also need an involved father who isn't just a paycheck. You work not just to support your family, but to be with it. I mean if you're just going to never be home to see your wife and children and just hand over your money, plus you're down to sex a couple of times a month, well what's the difference between that and being divorced? Well apart from being allowed variety in your sex partners of course...

So go carefully gentlemen. Go carefully.

8 - Beating Approach Anxiety – So Easy A Caveman Can Do It

February 28, 2010

I've had a few questions about approach anxiety recently. Of course being married I don't really have approach anxiety anymore, but my wife has it – usually if I return from an adult store with a mysterious black bag. She becomes quite anxious when I walk up to her with a bag that may or may not contain; a 14 inch dildo, industrial strength nipple clamps, enema kits (actually I can filch those from work) or funky condoms that look like they could double as mining equipment but are advertised as "for her pleasure." She's always relived to just see a magazine or a video.

Actually I find playing a porn video with the sound all the way off an excellent way to create an instant "man cave" in the basement and gain compliance with my wife keeping children out from under foot when exercising. The kids used to want to come down and watch me or dick around with 2 pound weights etc and generally ruin my routines. I'm down there becoming buff slowly but surely and wifey has given clear thumbs up to progress to date.

Anyway I digress – approach anxiety.

Back in The Time Before Writing, walking up to a fertile woman would have more than likely drawn the attention of the AMOG (Alpha Male Of the Group). I'm not talking about the high school quarterback here either; I'm talking about a pissed off thug with body scars and a nasty pointed stick.

So imagine you are the young warrior Throg walking up to the beautiful young Salette with a piece of meat you want to offer her... and some gazelle that you just killed. That's absolutely going to get the attention of Sal who is the mean bastard running the show, but a little bit older than you and who has a slight limp from that time a lion tried to make off with a baby. So as you walk across the camp to Salette with the gazelle, everybody knows what the hell is going down, and Sal stands up and starts walking towards you with his nasty pointed stick and a scowl. So young Throg, you got two choices.

1. FIGHT Sal and either lose and be badly hurt, or win and Salette becomes Throgette

2. FLIGHT run the frak away and try not to cry like a bitch.

As you walk across the camp towards Salette, your pulse is going to evaluate, blood pressure increase, palms sweat and time is going to pass slowly as all your senses gear up for either combat or running.

So fast forward to today. You're in a social gathering and across the room is Sally. She's gorgeous and sexy. There are a couple other guys in the room interested in Sally. As you walk towards her your pulse is going to elevate, blood pressure increase, palms sweat and time is going to pass slowly as all your senses gear up for either combat or running. Except the other guys don't have spears and if it gets violent the cops get called and they go to jail for a breather. Seems stupid now doesn't it. But it feels 100% real.

Approach anxiety is nothing more that your Body Agenda preparing you to deal with a Time Before Writing AMOG that never comes. It's all a terrible red herring to worry about. The solution is that when you see a girl you have interest in, to not even wait a second to make a move on her, just immediately plow ahead and introduce yourself and get the ball rolling. You do this to beat your body's reaction time in getting the whole fight or flight / approach anxiety thing up to speed. You have about a 3 second window before it kicks in. The longer you wait the worse it is.

The flip side to this reaction is confidence. And well all know how the ladies love confidence and how sexy confidence is. The reason for this is simple and fundamental. When a man with confidence walks up to them and just starts talking, and isn't displaying approach anxiety / fight or flight reactions… that can only mean one thing… he's the AMOG! Only the AMOG would be able to just walk up to a woman and start a sexual interaction and not be worried about a guy with a pointed stick running at him. And women are very much turned on by Alpha Male approaches. That's the way their Body Agenda is wired.

Again back in The Time Before Writing women had essentially no choice about who they had sex with. Salette's sexual options essentially boiled down to consensual sex with the winner of Throg vs. Sal, or non-consensual sex with the winner of Throg vs. Sal. The Time Before Writing is not a pretty place for a woman I confess. But it's honestly not that much different now as clearly hair pulling still makes vaginas tingle and romance novels are chock full of plot lines about how the daring Throg finally gets the evil Sal his comeuppance and somehow Throgette gets pushed up against a wall and just ravished by Throg on pages 87, 104, 127 through 132 and finally on 172.

The best solution – once again this point is so critical to nearly everything if you're a couch potato unhappy with your sex life – is attention to physical fitness and even picking up a martial art if you have to. The purpose is that by increasing physical ability, you are convincing your own Body Agenda that you can survive a physical fight with a Time Before Writing AMOG or at least make it enough of a pain in the ass to fight you that the imaginary AMOG doesn't force a fight.

So physical fitness, maybe a martial art if you really must, realize that your body reaction is just a Time Before Writing holdover and ignore it, and just make a move before the approach anxiety kicks in. Just make approaches until you realize that it's all just pre-performance butterflies and completely normal.

Go. Don't think. Just go.

9 - What To Do When Your Wife Won't Have Sex With You

March 7, 2010

Via email and comments I keep getting asked a variation on this question;

"How do I make my wife do (or be) XYZ?"

Also the questioners almost always want something that "works right away."

Well the first step in troubleshooting a wife that isn't working properly is to disconnect her from her power source and wait 30 seconds, then plug her back in and see if when she reboots that solves the problem. Often that solves the issue with some of the earlier Stepford models. Otherwise open up the back and manually pull out and switch the Soap Opera Module and the Sex Drive Module into each other's slots, then restart and clear the shoes and shopping cache and see if that frees up memory processing. If that fails call tech support and we never had this conversation.

Of course if you're still struggling with one of the quaint flesh and blood types, things are a little different. These ones have a voice activated interface where you actually have to talk to them to discuss what it is you want from the relationship.

Of course that all can fail and you can find yourself denied enough sexual expression in your relationship, while at the same time being also denied allowance to otherwise find satisfaction outside your relationship. That's a cruel situation and yes I believe you are being cheated out of what you signed up for. Then a struggling husband finds me somehow and they end up asking me for a magic bullet to make the wife turn red hot and willing.

I'm all out of magic bullets. I had three of them but I traded one for World of Warcraft gold in 2005, I was doing the dishes and lost the second down the sink and with the third I accidentally shot myself in my own ass. Sorry, my bad.

Anyway...

Assuming the wife has no medical/health issues nerfing her sexual desire in general, my basic theory is that if your wife isn't sexually interested in you, it's because she doesn't find you sexually attractive. I.e. she's a Sex Rank 7 and you're a Sex Rank 6.

You can beg, plead, reason, argue, make deals, promise, hope, pray, wish, dream, ask and cry with frustration to your wife about the sex life you have and it will likely make little difference. Oh sure she may make a token effort to have more sex, but after a week or two it will return to the baseline sex life you had. She's not into you.

The solution is not to see it as "her problem" and something she needs to change about her in order to fix things. She can't change this. Sexual attraction isn't a choice it's a response to stimulation. The solution is for you to become more sexually attractive. If you're a Sex Rank 6, you become a Sex Rank 7. Then go to 8. She will find it hard not to respond to you more sexually. You won't even be likely to need to have the conversation to ask her to do more sexual things or be more emotionally connected to you. She'll just respond.

Of course the one thing that I need to emphasize here is that actually increasing your Sex Rank isn't quick and it isn't easy. If for example you issue is that you weigh 240 pounds, and you really should be 180 pounds, that road to lose 60 pounds is not going to be overnight or effortless. If your issue is that you can't hold a job, turning that around can take 1-2 years before you find one, settle your crap down and get to a first promotion / better hours etc. If you issue is you dress like a slob, finding that extra $1-2,000 to transform a wardrobe can take a while to earn and spend. If you're terrible at keeping a house together, you may have a few years worth of DIY projects ahead of you.

As a rough guide give yourself a year per point of Sex Rank... i.e. 6 turning into a 7 is a year. Then 7 into 8 is a second year. It's a slow and gradual and serious effort process. There is no one killer move that makes her vagina explode with fluids at your approach. It's about you becoming a better man. Good sex is the consequence of being sexy.

Also I've said numerous times that the entire approach of becoming more sexy may in fact fail with your wife. You can turn from 6 to 7 to 8 and she may respond to that, or she may not. My hunch is that the majority of the time she will. After all she was into you enough to marry you, so there has to be some sort of baseline interest, and that interest should peak if you are the best version of you possible. I also expect that as you perk up your Sex Rank, she will follow your lead to keep pace. Ideally there isn't even a "fight night" where everything turns into a dramatic confrontation – you just up the sexy and she follows suit.

However, she may not respond positively and you will be faced with the possibility that the marriage will have to end in order to move onto the sex life you need and deserve. If it goes down the divorce route, you are still better off seeking new sex partners as an 8 than as a 6. So either way you will win from the process of making yourself more attractive to women.

Also by failing to take action and increase your sex appeal, you run the risk that your wife may simply take her own action against your own interest. She may simply divorce you or cheat on you. You may get to be a proud but unwitting non-biological father. Women like sex just as much as men do. If she is not having sex with you because she is not attracted to you, that does not mean she has a low sex drive. If you are less sexy than your wife and you plan to just coast along, do not be surprised if you find out one day that she has a lover she is passionately involved with. And you sure as hell don't offer to share her with anyone to try and keep her with you. That's like being in the express lane in the wrong direction. Chump be thy name.

Here's how it plays out:

If both husband and the wife take positive action, both partners become sexier and have a vibrant increase in their sex life.

If the husband takes positive action and the wife refuses to, the husband ends up moving onto hot new sex partners. The wife buys cats and hates the husband for divorcing her.

If the wife takes positive action and the husband refuses to, the wife gets to move on to new sex partners. The forlorn husband masturbates to the memories of his departed wife.

If both partners refuse to take positive action, the marriage stays stable. The husband becomes addicted to porn, and the wife becomes fatter and gives up shaving her legs.

So as cynical as my advice may seem, the only person you can really control is you. And as long as you take positive action, you will end up with a positive sexual outcome regardless of your wife's decisions and behavior.

Naturally there is no rush to an ultimatum. Divorce is amazingly serious with kids and houses and money and careers all tied up together. Unpicking all that is going to be a mess. But if you're basically being shorted on the love and sex front, you are ultimately being screwed over and sometimes you just have to see the whole thing as abusive towards you. You can't have an agreement for a fair exchange, do your part and not get your half of the exchange in return.

The other thing to consider is that when you're about 2-3 months in, your wife should be noticing some positive changes in you. Don't forget that marriage is a team sport. If you can prove that you're heading in a positive direction and have some momentum, she's quite possibly going to be your biggest ally in your quest.

Pickup Artist Game is all about Style. Married Game is all about adding Substance. Get some.

10 - Dominance and Submission in Marriage: The Captain and First Officer Model

March 13, 2010

The world we live in is quite removed from The Time Before Writing. For the modern world learning and understanding appropriate dominance and submission are key life skills for both sexes. Whether you are male or female I suggest you submit to your work supervisors male or female, and be dominant towards your work subordinates male or female. With your work peers you will likely have an ebb and flow of dominance and submission.

However in the context of marriage I believe for most of us a pattern of male dominance and female submission has a basis in Body Agenda. Women respond sexually to dominant men and they can become quite aggressive towards men that seek sexual access that do not evoke feelings of submission in them. The Body Agenda literally thinks "if he can't handle me, he can't actually protect me from anything." Often a woman will tear her husband apart over quite minor things seeking a reaction to correct her. If she doesn't get that correction she can become increasingly agitated with her man and progressively more extreme in efforts to force that reaction. The majority of drama queens are just seeking the king to finally show up and tell her to knock it off.

Again - I'm talking about one man and one woman with each other. I'm not talking about all men over all women. Nor am I saying all marriages have to work this way. Just that I believe most would run better for trying it. Many women actively seek domination in their sexual relationships.

As I've posted many times before, I'm not a particularly aggressive Alpha Male type guy by nature. Much of that stuff I've learned along the way over the last decade and in the last few years in particular. One of the things I was very careful to do when Jennifer and I married was to strive for equality between us, and I was quite careful to not be domineering over her.

The result of those good intentions was that often we'd grind to a halt in a deadlock of mutual submission. "What do you want to do?" "I don't know, anything is fine. What do you want to do?" Just repeat that conversational cycle for about ten years and you get the picture. I've often wondered in the last year how someone didn't just poach her from me early on by simply being assertive towards her and doing something dramatic like... I don't know, simply asking her out on a well planned date or something clever like that. I guess I am lucky.

Well, lucky and good... I don't mean to distract from the main thrust of this post, but Jennifer and I are each other's sexual first and we had been long distance in separate countries up until two weeks before our marriage. When we married I was basically unleashing a lifetime of pent up sexuality and generally quite assertive in getting sex and making sure she liked it. That first flurry of sex basically set the tone of the sex in our marriage and it's continued on that way. In retrospect I was doing the one very Alpha thing with her from the start of our marriage. That solves a multitude of non-Alpha displays in other areas.

About five years ago I started getting grumpier with some of our mutual submission deadlocks and just started saying what I wanted. Jennifer lapped it up. This was initially very confusing, I thought and felt acting like this was in fact offensive and waited for the response of anger and annoyance of being bossy. It never came. I shit you not.

Since then I've reprogrammed myself a great deal away from the idea that everything has to be perfectly equal and fair. I've come to realize that being submissive is something she actually gains an active enjoyment from. Some of that is social submission, some of that is sexual submission. It's only in the last year or two that I've found myself actively enjoying being dominant. I've given orders on and off for much longer, but felt quite weird about it at first, then felt neutral, but now can sometimes get physically turned on simply by requesting sexual submission.

Some of this is exceptionally simple everyday stuff. If we have four things that have to get done, Jennifer is great at defining the tasks, but if I step in and say "well lets both go and do A and B together because they are close together, then you go do C and I'll double back to here and do D" she positively beams simply because I made the decision and set direction. Likewise if she wants to go out to dinner, me deciding the place makes her happy.

We did grocery shopping together today. After we came out of the store I said I wanted coffee, I got an "oh that sounds good" and off we went. We went through McDonalds and got coffee and had a Filet-of-Fish each. I get a "this was a fabulous idea" from her. She's made happy by this. We did not cover this reaction in my Sociology of the Family course in college. Yeah... I have a degree in being non-dominant towards women. Waste of time and money. True story.

Anyway...

Jennifer is certainly not mindless. She's not sitting at my feet with a leash and collar as I write. She doesn't just sit around and wait for direction. She's actually one of the most competent people I know. I'm not going to spell out what she does for work, but I can assure you she is extremely talented and a vital resource for her company.

Over the last six months I've come to understand how our relationship works best and integrate the sense of wanting to be fair, but also define the element of dominance and submission. I'm come to understand it as being a Captain and First Officer relationship. And yes I first thought of this as a Star Trek metaphor (I don't dress up for conventions, I just like the shows) though it's basically standard for commercial airliners and military chain of command. As Wikipedia describes a First Officer...

"In commercial aviation, the first officer is the second pilot (sometimes referred to as the "co-pilot") of an aircraft. The first officer is second-in-command of the aircraft, to the captain who is the legal commander. In the event of incapacitation of the captain, the first officer will assume command of the aircraft.

Control of the aircraft is normally shared equally between the first officer and the captain, with one pilot normally designated the "Pilot Flying" (PF) and the other the "Pilot Not Flying" (PNF), or "Pilot Monitoring" (PM), for each flight. Even when the first officer is the flying pilot, however, the captain remains ultimately responsible for the aircraft, its passengers, and the crew. In typical day-to-day operations, the essential job tasks remain fairly equal."

I've always liked the dynamic on the Star Trek series between Captains and First Officers. It's always been quite apparent that the First Officer is always competent and skilled, and if anything happens to the Captain, they step into the role of being in command immediately. The Captains always listen, because sometimes the First Officer has a better idea than their own. Sometimes the First Officer actually overrules the Captain in a crisis and gives the crew an order, the Captain usually just trusts the First Officer isn't doing this to make trouble and runs with it. But at the end of the day... the Captain is the Captain and leadership comes from them, and final responsibility for the ship lies with them. If it all goes to hell the Captain is last off the ship.

My realization is that most wives want the First Officer job. Not Crewman Third Class, but not Captain either. They want to have a say and be heard, they want to be trusted, they don't want to be micro managed on decisions they are capable of making themselves, they can happily step it up into "having the bridge" when their husbands aren't available. They just would rather be the second in command and follow someone else's leadership and general direction.

The challenge for the husband is not to go into marriage as a Redshirt waiting for the deathblow. If that's what you expect, that's what you'll get. Also do not go into marriage and attempt to simply be a member of the crew. The wife will likely try and assume a First Officer role and that makes her the de facto Captain if the husband doesn't take that position. That may well piss her off. He can even do everything she says wants and asks him to do, and by submitting to her perfectly, that can actually anger and disappoint her more and more. Most men find this extremely confusing.

We have different areas that we specialize in and basically have complete control over. Sometimes I "have the bridge" and sometimes she does. But ultimately looking back over our marriage I can see that the majority of our direction and big decisions have been mine with Jennifer supporting me. I've not always been right. Sometimes I've been quite badly wrong. But even when I've been wrong, badly wrong, Jennifer somehow manages to stay supportive. I don't quite understand how she does that. I've come to be awed by that support, but I don't fully understand it. Must be a chick thing.

There's no violence. No screaming matches. There are roles, and trust and love. No threats or retaliations. No infliction of pain. Well... occasional light spankings. But we both enjoy that.

So... Captain and First Officer. That's my theory for male dominance and female submission in marriage. Maybe it's not right for your marriage, but in ours it really works for both of us. There are hardly any of those mutual submission battles anymore. I just decide to do what I want more often, and I know what she likes quite well and a good portion of the time I decide we do that. Upon the rare occasion she complains, I might reach for the verbal nuke... "Captains prerogative Number One."

One thing to watch for is other women picking up on your dominant sexual vibe. It does not hurt at all to think of your wife as your Number One. After all, that is ultimately what she is to you.

11 - The Dark Side Of Game

March 16, 2010

Let me tell you a tale about how I have some concerns about the dark side of Game...

We all know the story about the chick that has an abusive boyfriend. First she loves loves loves him, this guy is so special, he's so perfect, he's so different. She will not shut up about this guy.

And we all hate listening to her because we all know what is coming.

It starts as a raised voice. Then there's a push. Then there's yelling. Then the pushing becomes a shove. There's name calling and a slap. Then it's just hitting.

This is not the escalation of touch I like talking about.

Then she breaks free of him in a heroic effort. Puts her life back in order. Becomes stronger. Tells everyone how assured and certain of herself she is now. Then she meets a guy...

...he's so special, he's so perfect, he's so different. She will not shut up about this guy. And we all hate listening to her because we all know what is coming.

Thankfully some women really do break free from the cycle of abuse, but it's hard. How does anyone really bounce back from being beaten by someone that they love? I suspect most just send out a vibe into the world saying how they expect a man who touches their heart to destroy them as best he can. Then drip tears into their wounds and start the punishment over again more thoroughly until one of them breaks completely.

So what about you Mr. Man. Any lessons here for you? After all this is a male orientated blog.

What sort of vibe are you sending out into the world to attract women to you?

/Activate Sith Mode

Are you terrified of marriage? Or terrified of divorce? Does the idea of a marriage actually working actually scare you... after all you might relax your defenses and then one day discover yourself suddenly under a restraining order, the bank accounts empty and have to listen to the sound of her heels clicking off into the distance to meet her lover. You might drive past the house you paid for every day of the rest of your life and feel the twist of the knife of his car in your garage and pound the steering wheel in impotent frustration. Your fear is quite rational.

The kids might not be yours either. You might have to pay for the kids that aren't yours until they turn 18. Half, more than half of everything you earned and owned simply gone to the sound of a judges hammer like you're trapped in a dream about your own estate sale and you don't have a bidding paddle. Ramen noodles - hallowed be thy name.

Women are such heartless plotting bitches. They can have sex for money. Always scheming a way to destroy and suck the income from a man. They want it bigger and better and NOW. More than money, they want his marrow. They secretly smile to themselves as the lingerie vault slams forever like a tomb and thrill to his anguished cries of need for her to show a hint of desire towards him. Such pretty things are not for you.

The only way to deal with such predators is to become a predator yourself. Turn the tables, change the game, and load the dice in your favor. Crush the feelings you have for any of them and rub the nose of "the one" in the scent of ten other vaginas to prove you cannot be weak to the touch of a woman. Eat kryptonite for breakfast, after all what does not kill you makes you stronger.

Find them, hunt them, trap them, break them, r*** them.

Lie.

Lie until the lies you tell, you tell so well they are the truth.

Then when you win... a woman giving herself to you, fully, completely and passionately. Savor it. When you are finished with her, turn your back on her in the bed and cuss or elbow her away when she tries to cuddle. Make sure she is damaged for every other man she meets.

Hurt her.

Dear boy... I know all this sounds a bit harsh... but understand I tell you all of this as your friend. I don't want to see you making some of the same mistakes I've made. The same mistakes all men make. It's for the greater good. Be assured that women are the enemy of man. Let me teach you.

/Deactivate Sith Mode

So like I was saying... What do you really think about women? What are you projecting out into the world to attract to you? Is it helping? Is it truly what you want to experience from a woman?

There are good women out there. Ones that will love you, cherish you, support you, love you and gaze upon you glassy eyed as you get them with child. They will live with you, feed you, laugh with you, touch you, hearts break and hearts make with you.

They will fight for your marriage when you don't. They will carry the load for you, when you won't. In your darkest hour, they may be your light.

If you cannot find these women, maybe the problem is you.

"Lord Vader, it appears in your anger you killed her."

12 - Monogamy as a Sexual Strategy: My Wife Was Right All Along

April 4, 2010

Had a set of questions in a comment on "The Dark Side of Game." This turned into a long and quite personal post. I'm quite naturally good at marriage, but that's not the same as perfect. Read on.

"Cool blog. Athol, you seem to subscribe to the Cinderella model of male/female relationships i.e. man and woman can live happily ever after.

Studies abound that show that brain chemistry, while wildly active and effective at first, loses nearly all potency in approximately three years. Again, on a chemical level, lust turns to love, then to like then to roommates and often it goes downhill from there.

~55% of married men cheat and ~%45 of married women cheat. Their combined efforts implicate an ~80% chance of infidelity affecting marriage.

99% of all mammals are not monogamous. Are you still clinging to the Christian ideal? Just curious..."

-Bill

Hi Bill, no I don't have a fantasy outlook on marriage - there are clearly serious risks involved, but it is also possible to maintain a long happy relationship with an excellent upside. As a smart guy

I think I can affect the outcome. Choice of wife is paramount of course.

I would lean on the work of Dr Helen Fisher for the biochemistry of attraction. There are three quite different sets of biochemistry - the "in love" one which is quite erratic, the "pair bond" which tends to develop and strengthen over time, and "basic horniness" which is a diffuse all purpose desire for sex. If you lose the "in love" chemical surge, but fail to develop the pair bond, you will end up roommates and have relationship failure. But the two chemical markers are different and it isn't an either/or choice. It's possible to be both in love and pair bonded at the same time. I can assure you I still find my wife quite sexually arousing after 15 years together.

Cheating figures vary wildly, so it's very hard to know what percentage of marriages are affected. To be honest it's best to just accept that Sex Rank issues do not stop at the altar and that both partners need to maintain their attractiveness and interest in each other or risk relationship failure. Whether that comes via affairs or simple disbandment the outcome is the same.

Once you toss emotional affairs into the mix, I think basically all marriages probably have attachments to others outside the relationship as a natural hazard. How you and your partner negotiate these hazards is the question.

The most interesting question is whether or not I am still clinging to the Christian ideal. Actually one of the most difficult aspects of Christianity to me was the ideals of no sex before marriage et al. Honestly I really hated it and figured it made minimal sense for the modern age. In the historical context of no birth control it certainly made more sense, but not really for now. It was a factor in why I stopped believing.

After I stopped believing I very much explored non-monogamy on an intellectual level and put some gentle pressure on Jennifer to explore that in real life with me as well. We've had a very limited number of quite mild experiences with that more than ten years ago, but it simply became apparent that Jennifer was complying for me rather than her own interest and just didn't really want to do anything with anyone else but me. So all in all it was shelved as something we were not going to be doing. This was quite frustrating to me for a long time (I have a strong sexual impulse!), but not a deal breaker in the middle of a very happy marriage and life continued on.

After many years together I've had a few outside "opportunities" thrown my way. I probably could have converted on these with some basic confidence, but lacked the sort of PUA Game back then that would have assisted in those moments. I'm a natural for Marriage Game, not quite so much at PUA, though I know much more now than I ever did before. Most of what I know now about PUA is me trying to reverse engineer why I am a marriage natural.

In retrospect I've come to realize and appreciate the way the story arc would have played out if I had followed up using PUA Game "correctly" and seduced a few women on the side... Jennifer would know. I know she would know, no matter how well I covered my tracks. Right now I'd probably be in a shitty marriage, or more likely divorced, paying child support and having to work a lot harder for a lot less sex than I'm getting now. I may well still be blogging, but this would be a very different blog. I'd not really be over Jennifer either, I'd miss my kids. In short the non-monogamy outcome would have been a lot worse for me than the monogamy outcome has been. Plus I'd unbelievably hurt her. I just don't need a theological argument for that to justify my thinking.

In retrospect I have unwittingly dodged some marriage ending bullets by having been a little clumsy with women. If you want the Mystery Method explanation... I can waltz to C3 and stumble historically at the transition to S1. The face-palm is realizing that all I really needed to do at those moments was say "Let's find someplace private and talk about how many orgasms you'd like." My basic issue is that I relate very well to women, work almost exclusively with them (I'm a nurse) and my emotional connections can progress quite quickly and get quite tangled. It's the downside if you like to be passionate, sexy and a good listener. Both Jennifer and I are aware of this much better now and we talk these issues out more. It's quite diffusing of these situations to bring them into the light rather than let them continue in secret.

Having been though multiple cycles of being completely centered on Jennifer, and having any sort of emotional / romantic pull to another person, I've just come to the understanding that I enjoy life better and have more enjoyable sex with her when I'm centered better on her. At this point if she were to suddenly express an interest in swinging or something similar I would be concerned... I've read too many horror stories where good marriages collapse when one half of the couple completely activates on the lover after only a single sexual experience and it's basically game over from that point. Seems a terrible risk to take for an orgasm. I'm quite humbled and awed that Jennifer has taken this all with such good grace. I'm not sure I would if the situations were reversed. (Yes that's a double standard I know.)

I see monogamy as a sexual strategy rather than a moral requirement. Obviously another sexual strategy is being promiscuous. As truly horrible as it sounds even rape is a sexual strategy to propel your genes into the next generation. Obviously all the different sexual strategies have different pros and cons, and in the case of rape a major con is the very strong and very appropriate social and legal sanctions that go with it. I just don't have the need for images of hellfire to justify the benefits of the monogamous strategy; the outcomes seem to be enough of a justification as it is. If I cheat on my wife, there's no God to see me doing it... I'd just risk damaging the best thing I have going for me... for us. Plus I'd damage my kids, which in turn damages my ability to have them propel my genes into the generation after them.

My major concern for other people is that pursuing the promiscuity strategy is not nearly as casual as it may appear on the surface. Mating with someone results in a major neurological and endocrine event designed to bond you to that person. Sometimes those links can be near permanent off of only a single mating, sometimes it takes more, but ultimately mating is designed on a biological level to bond us to the partner we are with. We're all familiar with reading about the Facebook Effect of old flames reigniting with outrageous passion after even decades apart. The bonding is real.

And yes, I can view an act of cheating as a simple EPC (Extra Pair Copulation) with the best of them. I get it. It's a sexual selection strategy at work.

But I just can't help but wonder if having multiple hook ups, single night lays, pump and dumps or whatever your term is, just damages our ability to properly bond to the person we decide to marry. Damages our ability to have the depth of the possible sexual connection with the one person we finally settle on.

The old standby advice from the PUA community in getting over a bad case of Oneitis is to FTOW – Fuck Ten Other Women – then see how you feel about the girl you had a terrible crush on. My question is – never mind the original girl, are you even going to be capable of feeling anything like that again for anyone? Or will you simply be too jaded to care?

As I've said before, a married guy learning PUA sort of game is going to eventually face a test. I passed mine not too long ago and that's about all I want to say on that front. Being honest though, it was much harder than I thought it would be and I'm turning 40 this month. I can't imagine the struggle younger guys would have with it. I don't know if I would have passed it when I was 25. I probably would have ruined everything I have now. It's sobering.

The irony of my views on monogamy now as compared to my younger self is not lost on me. The switch from a Christian desiring non-monogamy, to an Atheist enjoying monogamy is somewhat counter-intuitive, but there we go. Maybe I'm just older now.

So anyway… life continues on. My wife continues to amaze and delight me. The kids are of the pleasing variety. I am happy and content. More so now than ever before. The sex is outstanding.

The old joke is actually true. Monogamy really is a type of wood.

13 - Oh Nice, Now My Wife Is Gaming Me Back

April 10, 2010

By and large writing this blog is a great DHV (Display of Higher Value), so generally speaking it all works in my favor of upping my Sex Rank in Jennifer's eyes. I've done a lot of writing, there's a positive response from others including other female readers rocking out my Preselection as well. All in all it's a good boost for me.

Now I can write just fine, but my proof reading skills suck. For those following the story closely, you know that Jennifer does the final proof reading before I publish my posts. I've been reading widely for decades on sexuality, but now that she's reading my stuff she's been coming across the key concepts more seriously. And she's naturally smart, so she's learning... and adapting.

Today I got my first proper taste of my own medicine handed back to me...

"Dear..."

That's how 99% of Jennifer's baby shit tests start, so I'm ready for it. Plus "dear" isn't pronounced just "dear", it's pronounced "deeeeeeeeeeaaaaaaaaarrrrrr" with lightly fluttering eyelashes and a "so cute" front reverse hand clasp and slight body rocking and one heel lifted off the ground. It sounds freaking awful I know but she actually pulls this look off amazingly well. Two weeks ago she was carrying daughter #2's backpack and was mistaken for a 5th grader from behind by a teacher, which is quite possibly the happiest moment of her 37 years the way she tells the story.

Anyway... she is pulling off "the cute" I'm usually mildly amused by this I also know that a request is going to be forthcoming... but today she ups the ante with a new spin.

"Deaaaaaaarrrrrrr...

.....I need an Alpha Male...."

...

Ah Ma Gawd.... I hate going to Home Depot.

14 - Sexy Move: Biotone Advanced Therapy Massage Cream

April 16, 2010

A while back I played with the idea of turning into a massage therapist and attended an open house at a massage school. I didn't actually apply, but I did shop in the little school store and basically stumbled upon the most fantastic lotion for ~~handjobs~~ massages.

The magic lotion is Biotone Advanced Therapy Massage Cream. Comes in either an 8oz pump thingy or a gallon bottle. You can find it at Amazon.com, but is cheaper from the manufacturer. We usually get a gallon every couple of years and refill a smaller bottle and it never seems to go bad. (no paid links, it just rocks)

We often ensure that I get lots of ~~handjobs~~ massages when Jennifer is in that time of the month when she likes giving ~~handjobs~~ massages. Sometimes I lie on my back and I get a lovely ~~handjob~~ massage, sometimes with her on top of me and sometimes she lies on her back with me over the top of her and I get a nice ~~handjob~~ massage that way. Though honestly that way is a little messy and the ~~cumshot~~ lotion goes everywhere, but it's non greasy and cleans up well.

Also as a side benefit, it's good for handjobs. So it's win-win.

(Edit: We switched to the Biotone Gel, it's even better!)

15 - Don't Destroy Your Sex Rank By Stupid Educational Choices

April 20, 2010

One of the more obvious things that make men sexy is having a coherent career. Whatever it is in particular isn't all that vital, as long as the man can show some kind of general story arc of making more money and generally gaining more power in his work environment.

Money isn't everything, but below a certain level of income, it sure feels like it's everything. When all is said and done, more money is generally better than less money. All things being equal the guy with a $100,000 income is going to go home with the pretty girl, and the guy making $25,000 gets to go home with her designated ugly fat friend aka "The DUFF."

This is an incredibly harsh way of looking at the world, but tell me it isn't the way it all plays out time and time again. Once upon a time having an income was all a guy needed to have in order to land a wife and she was completely dependent on him for that income. Times have changed and generally women earn similar incomes to men, but having a decent income still rates as an important signal of social worth.

We all don't get to be CEO's or astronauts, but as long as you aren't failing by ending up working retail, serving coffee or flipping burgers when you're age 30+, you're generally doing ok. To be sure some professions have a generally higher status than others, but what you do may not be as important as how you do it. You may be better off being an amazing teacher as opposed to a really awful lawyer for example.

One of the ways you can seriously damage your overall earning power and career arc is by being stupid in your education. You pretty much can't hurt yourself by your high school choices other than getting crappy grades, but once you're at the college level you can cripple yourself for years to come by bad choices.

Before you go to college – know that you are being sold a ticket to an outcome. The college doesn't care about the outcome; they only care about the sale of the ticket. So if the college can convince 500 people to enroll and graduate from Tulip Arranging, earning $60,000 per student, but only 2 jobs for Professional Tulip Arrangement exist and 498 people end up with a completely useless degree... well that's not really the college's problem. Well it might make the college business department build a statue of a giant Tulip with the $30,000,000 revenue and they will make damn sure that the brochures for the next class will be extra glossy.

Then the poor saps that graduated from Tulip Arranging have $45,000 worth of loans and Starbucks is hiring. They can't afford to return to college ever again, and there we go. Trapped serving coffee until they die. Trying to meet women when you're in debt and serving coffee has got to be the suck.

The problem is that a large number of college degrees / majors don't seem to be for anything other than filling out the coffers of the college. See, if you go through med school, nursing school, law school etc, all those schools are a direct line to having an actual job at the end of it. If you go through med school, it's pretty damn obvious that you better work your ass as a doctor at the end of school. That's the whole point. But if you do a degree in English, or History, or Psychology or basically any of the liberal arts degrees, there is no direct line to a job. You can complete you entire degree and still not know what the hell you want to do at the end of it.

Then you head out into the world and work for a bit and discover what you do like, and you may or may not have to head back to school to do that. All in all this turns into the most appalling waste of time and money right in your most fertile and attractive spouse seeking years.

Given the choice between a 25-26 year old male that has a smart education, and has been working in that field for a few years and had a minor promotion, or a 25-26 year old male that has a useless degree and is serving coffee, it's a no brainer what a savvy female is going to be more interested in. And by savvy I mean perky tits.

And let's not discount not even going to college. Plumbers, Electricians, Carpenters etc can all make WTF good money without even going to "higher" education. Just have a plan and play it out. Sometimes the "smart people" can make appalling decisions while the supposedly less smart people just have more common sense and finish strong. That's $400 to stop the leaky pipe on a Sunday for an hour's work. Think about that.

If you want to learn about Tulip Arranging, do it on your own time as a hobby. But don't waste tens of thousands of dollars and years of your life educating yourself for a job that may or may not be there, and may pay crappy money when you get there.

16 - Sex During Pregnancy and Married Man Game

May 4, 2010

I got asked a question via email about what's the biological basis for how sex in pregnancy plays out. The short answer is I know in a vague general sense, but pregnancies are so variable that giving individual advice is all but impossible.

Let's come at it from the other side of the equation first. The clutch-the-pearls and cut to commercial dramatic insight is that one of the most likely times for a husband to cheat on his wife is during her pregnancy. This makes perfect sense in that the biological point of sex for the man is to get the woman pregnant. Once she's actually pregnant its "Mission Accomplished" and being the cads that we are the biological cross hairs start looking for other targets. Like her sister. Or the wife next door. Or a babysitter. Or any of the 53 women he accidentally messaged on Ashley Madison.com.

So one possible counter tactic for the pregnant woman to keep Mr. Naughty around home base and not throwing his dick into an unsanctioned orifice, is to actually become quite exceptionally horny. See, if he's drained and limp from constant playtime he's essentially disarmed and while he can do a fly by over foreign soil he can't actually get into a sortie and fire any missiles. Plus all those pony rides are quite bonding of him to her thanks to Oxytocin.

The other thing that happens in general is that women lose some attraction to Alpha types and gain some attraction to Beta types. The reason for that is quite simple, the Alphas tend to come with better genes and at this point she's got whatever male deposited genes she has inside her already so that avenue of interest is a done deal. However the raising of the baby is more easily done by a nice Beta Daddy. Someone who will hold a job, help out around the house, play with the baby and generally not drink beer while farting heavily into the good couch every night.

I'm sure you all know a few women who got knocked up by their Bad Boy boyfriends that they just couldn't get enough off, suddenly have this 180 degree horrified change of heart when Mr. Motorcycle No Helmet made it plain that diaper changing was a completely female orientated task in his book. Then they have to shop for a new man with 8 pounds of screaming baggage and stretch-marks. (We all saw that coming by the way; you were the last to know.)

The trouble is that beyond a general increase in sexual interest, and a move towards appreciation of the Beta Male Traits, that individual pregnancies are as I said so variable that individualized advice is near impossible. Even for the same woman each pregnancy can be vastly different. Sometimes there is terrible morning sickness, others a wave of mild nausea. Some women become highly sexually aggressive, others find it wanes, some become moody and annoyed, others turn into a Zen like calm, some have a lot of pain and discomfort, others feel great up until the final few weeks.

So in some senses my advice is just "see how it goes." For the husband though, in general don't neglect the value of some of the more Beta sort of things. The married father gets far better points for helping out around the house than simply being someone's boyfriend does. Obviously you shouldn't give away the entire Alpha line of goodies, that way leads to masturbation and defeat, but if you can't show some willingness to Beta Up over a pregnant wife you're going to brand yourself negatively to all women that meet you into the future.

If you're leaning towards bad boy and she's in her 6th month, and you leave one Saturday morning with a motorcycle and come back with something with four doors and two new car seats from Wal-Mart "one for your car one for mine", she will likely openly sob into your chest clutching onto your shirt. Then she will talk about that moment for the next... well for the rest of her life. The only thing you have to remember is something that she wore that day. So when she tells that story twenty two years later you can say something like "Oh yeah I remember that day, you were wearing those green dangling earrings, the whole time you were crying into my chest I couldn't help thinking how nice they looked."

Then she'll be stunned that you remembered her most awesome moment better than she did after twenty-two years. Then any form of questioning about how you remembered can be simply cut off with "Well of course I remember... *it was our baby."* Then kiss close and f-close as soon as possible. As in immediately. As in stop everything and pull her to the bedroom and start taking her clothes off. Half cooked dinner be dammed, order take out later.

Hmmm kind of wandered off a little there...

Anyway, for the ladies reading. Beyond medical needs requiring you to abstain from sex, you would be utterly foolish to reduce or otherwise be unexcited about sexing up your husband while pregnant. In many ways your behavior in your first pregnancy is going to set the tone for the rest of your marriage. If you turn into a total bitch demanding to be catered to, that will very likely continue into the rest of your marriage. If pregnancy is your excuse not to have sex with your husband, that will likely continue into the rest of your marriage. Make him feel like the baby is more important than him during the pregnancy and he'll quietly and permanently resent his displacement for the rest of the marriage. This will basically self-destruct things on you at the seven year itch mark.

On the other hand if you find yourself grabbing the occasions that vaginal sex is possible, or when you're less horny but not completely crappy offering handjobs and blowjobs. Just asking for help in an even tone of voice rather than wailing for attention. Trying to make the experience as shared as it can be, (and I get that it's not really shared, but do try and cut him "into things" rather than "out of things") then that will probably carry over into the rest of your marriage too.

And Spoons. Spoons is a great position towards the end.

17 - Long Distance Relationship = Emotional Marathon

May 14, 2010

I have had a couple of questions about how Jennifer and I stayed together before we married. For those following we had a three year, three month courtship, during which we were actually in the same country physically together for a total of three months.

The short answer is I have no clue; I was out of my mind.

The long answer is;

(1) Meet girl
(2) Fly back to New Zealand
(3) Masturbate furiously
(4) ????
(5) Get Married!

I know that's not terribly helpful, but that's about the truth of it.

Okay something more I guess. We basically both just activated on each other and parting was awful. We had no contact with each other for a few months after I went back until she sent me a package thingy. After we got to talking it became quickly apparent that if we were to ever be together in the same country, it would require a huge commitment from one person to make the move, and that naturally suggested the other person also make a huge commitment.

So we were talking marriage before the first kiss.

I visited her and her family for Christmas for seven weeks and after about 2-3 weeks together I proposed. She came out to New Zealand and met my family the following Christmas. About a year later we married and I moved here.

But yes... this was a horrible time in many ways. Just a dull ache that gnawed away at everything. No email, no Skype, a handful of expensive phone calls, just lots of letters that took weeks to travel across the Pacific. Just an emotional marathon. Actually being married just seems like easy mode after all that.

Jennifer is the biggest risk I have taken in my whole life. I left everything, my family, my country, and my friends. It's paid off though. We're home.

18 - Comfort Building Rituals

May 21, 2010

I tend to get up earlier than Jennifer on the weekend. By which I mean her lazy fine ass stays in the bed as long as humanly possible. Actually it sounds a little like a shit test, but it's really not. She needs her sleep and there's nothing she really needs to be doing early on a Saturday anyway. Let's face it, she does her Wonder Woman routine all week and I wear her out as well. She really doesn't need me screeching like a newborn on the weekend mornings.

So usually I time a breakfast or coffee run for about when she is getting up. Sometimes it's fancy stuff, but usually not. Just a good cup of coffee and something to eat. It's both predictable and a little random. Chicks dig that.

Just like finding food in The Time Before Writing I've gone out and hunted and successfully returned to her with some. Admittedly bagels are only dangerously aggressive on rare occasions, so a little of the warrior flair is lost, but it's quite symbolic anyway. So she gets her sleep and I get to do a very comfort building little ritual for us. Jennifer is a generally upbeat person, but this really does make her feel good and it sets the mood for the rest of the day.

And importantly... no one bugs me for a couple of hours on Saturday mornings.

19 - Fitness Tests and My First Relationship Implosion

May 24, 2010

Periodically women Fitness Test (aka Shit Test) men. This can be quite purposeful and conscious testing, or it can be extremely unconscious testing that just springs up from nowhere. Suddenly she just *feels* something negative and the man must *do something* to alter the way she *feels* to positive. Typically these tests start fairly small, but over time they can grow larger and more demanding. The obvious intervention here is for the man to jump up and comply with her request and that does appease her... at first.

The problem lies in that Fitness Testing is the social equivalent of a sonar ping to determine social status. In general those of lower social status defer to those of higher social status. Women are hypergamous in their sexual attraction, so they are seeking their mate to be higher social status rather than lower. So when the male suddenly jumps up and complies with her request and seeks to appease her, he is deferring to her and demonstrating lower social status relative to hers. So while her minor inconvenience for the moment is taken care of, she becomes less happy with him because she finds him less attractive.

I first really ran into Fitness Tests with my first serious girlfriend Mary. It started off small, first she was late... and I tolerated it. Then she was nagging... and I listened. Then something about me wasn't quite right... and I changed it. Then she was really late... and I tolerated it more. Then we had to go to this horrible dance club... and I dragged myself there. Then we could do this and not that... I said ok. She nagged on and on and on and it just seemed to endlessly build.

In the end I simply wasn't prepared for any of this. I stuck to my game plan of being nice and helpful and after three months of being slowly sliced up and kissed... I flipped out completely and just dumped her. Then I was very sad for about 18 months getting over her. For those kind readers who periodically ask where the hell I was twenty years ago with the info I have on the blog... well that's where I was twenty years ago. Dumping my girlfriend in frustration and just bawling about it. A Kodak Moment...

Honestly if I knew everything back then that I know now, Mary and I might still be together. I think there was real love there on both sides, just she tested and I failed. In the end when I bumped back on her and stood my ground I did it way too hard and destroyed the relationship. Probably all I really needed to do early on is swat her on the ass a couple times and tell her to stop being a brat. Tease her back a little. In the aftermath she admitted she had been testing, testing purposely, but was to hurt too try again for fear of me nuking the relationship again. We both did wrong.

Of course that's all the road not taken and I just hope life played out well for her anyway. No clue where she is these days. I did try hunting for her on Facebook a while back, but... well you try and find a single "Mary" among the millions, lotsa luck with that lol.

So anyway... some painful lessons back in the day. Fortunately I've since learned to give a few playful swats on the ass and tease back a little. That's seriously about half the battle right there.

20 - What It Means When A Wife Says "I'm Bored."

May 30, 2010

There's something about the rattle of a rattlesnake that immediately brings your attention in sharp focus. It's a warning that bad things are about to happen if you don't stop whatever it is that you are doing and change course. Wives also have a rattle, it goes something like this...

"I'm bored."

On the surface that doesn't really get many guys attention, mainly because guys tend to solve their own problems of boredom so easily. We can just watch sports, play a video game, have sex or watch a YouTube video of a little kitty taking on a snake. We're all set... holy crap there's one of a baby in an awesome Ironman suit as well.

Ah.... see what I mean, guys can fill that void so easily. My bad... anyway, come back and we'll continue...

However...

When a woman says "I'm bored" though, you have to remember that most have a submissive element to their personality in relation to a male love interest. Meaning they actually get stimulation from being submissive to a man. The word "stimulation" is carefully chosen, it's not so much pleasure or enjoyment as the right sort of thing to activate their sexual interest. So what she is basically saying when she says "I'm bored" is "I'm not getting my submissive itch scratched, I'm kind of sitting around waiting for you to make something happen so I have to react to it and do something."

Or put another way, "I'm bored" = "I need a dominant male."

So... does that phrase sound a lot more like a warning sign that bad things are about to happen if you don't stop whatever it is that you are doing and change course? It should. When a wife is bored she's basically announcing a need for stimulation by a male being dominant towards her.

The first and most common way to get that need met is by trying to force the issue by creating a Fitness Test for you to bump back on her. She's being not so much a "bitch", just under stimulated and is just trying to create stimulation. When you pass the test and act dominantly towards her, she's getting her submissive itch scratched which is what she wants.

It's very rare that a woman knows herself well enough to realize on a logical level that she is feeling the need to be submissive and express that rationally and be pleased when her husband dominates her on cue. Most women find that having to say they need to be dominated "just ruins it" when he complies. He's just meant to know and do it, the phrase "I'm bored" is about as far as they go on the hinting before they start getting into feeling like they are the one running the game, rather than the game being run on them.

The other way a wife can get her boredom cured with a dominant male fix is pretty simple. She can find another man to excite her. Most often they still love their husbands, he's just... boring. They probably don't even mean to go looking for another guy, just one thing lead to another and it's exciting and the Dopamine pathways are getting all lit up inside their head. Pretty soon they are addicted to the flirty texts, emails and phone calls. You sure as hell want to interrupt that before they meet and do something physical.

So you need to keep things up on the Alpha Male / Dominance front for wives that respond to being submissive.

So as soon as you hear that cry of "I'm bored", know that no matter how happy you are in that moment and how well you think things are going between you... things are in fact dangerously bad. You can probably say to yourself, "Oh really? But we have this, and that, and I give her everything she could ever want and we don't fight or anything. Things are great." No they aren't. She's bored. I'll finish with a line that isn't exactly 100% guaranteed to happen, but it rhymes so it will stick in your head and you'd better remember it when you hear her say "I'm bored" to you....

If you're boring, she's whoring

21 - Fatherhood vs. Sexual Selection Failure

June 20, 2010

It's Father's Day, so obviously I'm meant to dredge up some sort of platitude about fatherhood that makes everyone feel all warm and fuzzy about fatherhood.

Nah... Sex Rank and the Body Agenda are too brutal for that.

So let's compare two guys to each other. The first is a "lowly Beta" with not much going for him other than a rather dull 4 wife. He's only ever had sex with her and together they have a couple of funny looking kids. The second is a master of Game and attractive to boot. Sex with approximately 120 women lifetime total. Smart as a whip, he dodges marriage and having children. Well, except for a near miss where a girlfriend got pregnant and he straight up told her to go fuck herself. She aborted the baby in the aftermath.

Well, according to the tenets of evolutionary psychology, only one of these guys is any good at sex. That's right, the lowly ugly Beta that has a couple of funny looking kids. Mr. Studly has a score of zero. He's a sexual selection failure. Technically he's an Omega Male based on his results.

Your Body Agenda doesn't care how many times you have sex. Your Body Agenda doesn't care how many women you sleep with. Your Body Agenda doesn't care how good looking the women you sleep with are if they aren't fertile. All that matters is baby making results and then having those babies go on and make more little babies and so on and so on. Sex is not the goal, it's simply a means to an end.

So anyway... this whole marriage and fatherhood plodding along thing. It's dull as can be some days no question. There are risks and pitfalls, but if you pay attention and play smart you can vastly increase the odds in your favor. For almost all of us it is the winning strategy for sexual selection.

Plus my wife makes me sandwiches.

22 - I Love You But I'm Not In Love With You = Another Guy On The Radar

June 27, 2010

Let's start with the very quick summary of Dr. Helen Fisher's work of three separate "love" body systems. All peer reviewed, shoving people in MRIs to look at their brains, lab tests for hormone levels yada yada yada.

In love = Dopamine based excitement / OCD like mental obsession on person of desire. The addition of Game understanding is that Alpha Traits compliment this process. (As an aside, SSRI anti-depressants routinely suppress this entire love system. Suggest extreme caution in using them.)

Pair Bond = Oxytocin / Vasopressin based emotional bonding and closeness. The addition of Game understanding is the Beta Traits compliment this process.

Sexual Drive = Testosterone based all purpose generic horniness towards the opposite sex. Physical fitness compliments this process.

The thing is women don't just leave a man they have a pair bond with because he's not Alpha enough. The leave him because another man enters the picture and they have "in love" feelings for him and they get the Dopamine OCD thing happening about the new guy.

When a woman tells a man ILYBINILWY (I Love You But I'm Not In Love With You) that means 9 times out of 10 there is a guy she is in love with that has entered the picture. ILYBINILWY is female code for some combination of "I'm leaving you for him", "I'm thinking about having sex with him", "I'm having sex with him but I want to live with you still is that ok?" and "I think I might be pregnant and don't know whose baby it is."

A woman can have minimal "in love" feelings the husband she is pair bonded to and just coast along for YEARS with no apparent cause for concern. I know of marriages where the wife clearly routinely craps all over her Beta husband and has done so for years and years but the marriage continues on unabated anyway. It is of course quite easy to be faithful if no one else wants to have sex with you.

But once a new man enters the picture that flips her Dopamine on, things can unravel between a wife and her overly Beta husband very quickly. The OCD like effects of the Dopamine response can overwhelm the strength of the pair bond. The woman gets torn between the two men she is chemically drawn too. It's not an easy emotional state to survive in for long. ILYBINILWY is also female code for some combination of "I have no clue how to make this decision", "Are you going to fight for me?"

As a final thought and adjustment to some of the bulk of this post: There is a growing sense of entitlement in women that their marriage relationship will be magically "in love" forever. Older women tend to not expect this so much and generally just stick with a boring Beta husband unless someone actively starts trying to game them and hooks them. Younger women feel far more entitled to this though, and they may simply begin to actively search for someone that excites them without a specific event.

Plus for my female readers, the core of this post "in love" vs. pair bond works exactly the same way for men too. Be advised to show cleavage and leave no question in his mind that you're good in the sack. At the heart of things, this is what men want from marriage and how they experience love and pair bond to you. The rest is just details.

23 - Beware Of Asking For Marriage Advice From Close Friends

July 7, 2010

All marriages have rough spots where things aren't working as well as they could. For the most part it is pretty normal to have ups and downs. It's also not unusual to talk about things with an outside person to gain perspective on what's going on in the relationship.

However in the downs be careful about who you confide in about your marriage. If you're a man and you share things with a female friend, that can turn into a bridge towards an emotional entanglement that diverts energy away from the marriage. Odds are you're not actually going to share this stuff with an unattractive female friend that you have no passing interest in…. am I right?

…yeah I thought so.

Repeat after me… "I never meant for this to happen, we just started talking to each other and one thing led to another and now we're in love. I never meant for this to happen. I'm so sorry." That's your defense line according to the emotional affair script. Use it, live it, love it. You can also use the "we're soulmates" line as well.

Likewise if you start sharing the woes with your male friends, this can easily turn into a huge display of weakness. Let's face it, if your wife is halfway attractive all your male friends will have at least a passing natural impulse to have sex with her. Most will have her very much on their radar just through simple propinquity. This is all very normal and expected.

So anyway, if you start spilling the tale of woe to these guys that know your wife and secretly want to screw her, three things can possibly happen...

1. They actually respect you and your marriage and give good advice designed to support the marriage and improve things. It's awesome if you can find a friend with ED like this.

2. They offer reasonable advice but basically pump you for information on her and then use those insights to better run their own game on her and try and backdoor on you. To the chump asking for advice, Point 2 advice looks just like Point 1 advice - it looks helpful.

3. They actively discourage you about marriage and recommend divorce. This easily clears you out of the way and creates the opening with your ex-wife that they "Tried talking sense into the dumb bastard" and "I'm appalled that he walked out on you", then "Can I help you with anything?" which leads naturally to "This going to sound corny but I've always wanted you, I just never made a move because Chump was a friend."

A year later he marries your ex-wife and moves into your home. Meanwhile you pay child support and pound your hands on the steering wheel of the car as you watch him flip burgers on your grill in the backyard.

Actually there's an easy progression from Point 1 to 2 to 3. I'm not saying they planned it or anything... it all started off as an attempt to help. Remember Point 1? That was a real attempt to help except you didn't listen / screwed it up. See, somehow it's your fault for being a chump.

So anyway, if you ask your buddy why the hell he stole your wife from you, you know exactly what he'll say... "I never meant for this to happen, we just started talking to each other and one thing led to another and now we're in love. I never meant for this to happen. I'm so sorry."

It actually sounds believable too. It's believable because they really believe it to be true. Though that's small comfort when he's using your grill and she won't shut the hell up about how good his hamburgers are.

The moral of the story is if you want to talk about your marriage with an outside person, find someone that is an objectively disinterested party. That could be a counselor, a mentor, your parents, or an online forum even. Also you can do it as a couple and that creates a united front rather than displaying weakness.

/Irony ON

Or if you must confide in a male friend about your marriage issues, at least talk to one that's completely hopeless and clueless about women and has no helpful advice at all, rather than the friend that understands women, has genuine skill and can charm the pants off nearly anyone.

/Irony OFF

See what I mean? There's not usually a good close male friend option to go to about this stuff.

Or put another way... if you cut your thumb open on a fish hook, would you just hang your arm over the side of the boat and trail your bleeding hand in the water?

24 - Live Long And Prosper

July 22, 2010

It's abundantly clear from a pure biological standpoint that humans are not designed to be purely monogamous. A reading of any of the basic evolutionary psych primers will get you to that understanding. (A cheat sheet version of Sperm Competition and Concealed Ovulation is a reasonable starting point at Wikipedia.)

From a biological perspective, both men and women appear to be built for a primary hormonally pair bonded relationship plus opportunistic sex outside that relationship.

Monogamy is a social adaptation that is somewhat in conflict with our Body Agenda. Our body is happy to hook up into a primary relationship, but it also keeps on the outlook for something tasty and proximal of the opposite sex. And yes, even if what's at home is tasty too.

So while we are not exactly designed for monogamy, it is a remarkably effective long term strategy as a building block for a society to use to advance. It is somewhat counter intuitive to our individual sexual desires, but I've previously argued that men in particular benefit from monogamy.

And likewise, we are not particularly perfectly designed for other modern social adaptations either. Things that spring to mind are; democracy, capitalism, the rule of law, science, medicine, education, standing in line, the Internet, driving, city apartment dwelling and most obviously... dealing with an ample food supply.

I mean if someone was designing humans from scratch to do all that, we'd all be speaking Vulcan.

25 - Sexy Move: Get Her To Cook You Breakfast

July 25, 2010

I did a quick shopping run this morning for hash browns, sausage and waffles. I do love a cooked breakfast. Before I left I told Jennifer where I was going and what I was buying and asked if she wanted coffee as well (Medium Hazelnut Light and Sweet - know your woman's preferences) and I got the gooey eyed look from her. But then it's early morning and she needed to wash her face properly before I could get a heart-all-fuzzy look.

Then I made my move... I pawed at her leg like a puppy wanting something. She laughed and said she'd cook.

"Yay! Being playful gets me what I want! Plus you need to get up anyway."

So off I go, collect the goodies and return home. She's up, teeth brushed and pony tailed (grrrrrowl, let me adjust myself baby) and without the morning breath keeping her tight lipped she kisses better.

Then I guess I just plain get underfoot by planning the breakfast that I asked her to cook. But we're talking and having fun. I end up deciding I have to leave the kitchen or just Alpha her out of the job, so I decide to back off and let her do it.

So I announce I'm clearing out and we have one last kitchen cuddle. She's snuggly his morning. As we break apart I purposely guide one of her hands into my crotch and say "What? Hey! Oh come on!" in mock surprise and outrage.

I'm ordered out of the kitchen by way of an out stretched arm holding a spatula like Babe Ruth calling his shot, but she's beaming and beautiful as she cooks breakfast.

The kids scarf down the eggs, sausage, waffles and hash browns like velociraptors deciding there might not be enough to go around. I have no idea where they learned that behavior. Anyway, the most important thing is that you must NOM NOM NOM NOM NOM, BURRRRRPPPP! SECONDS! NOM NOM NOM NOM! and once you have mastered that you'll have no problems with a wife.

In a bit there will be kitchen clean up and I'll mention in passing that Jennifer was a nice mommy and a good wifey this morning.... that's like a big red easy button that leads directly to her Vagina Tingle Cortex....

26 - If Women Are Naturally Submissive, Dominance Doesn't Need To Be Forced

August 4, 2010

Via "Hidden Leaves" (Blog)

"I didn't even know that your wife had a career. So it really piqued my interest to read about your debate about leadership in your marriage. I face a similar struggle myself. Our marriage is often too equal and therefore a perpetual power struggle. I would be very interested in your experiences in this realm. Other bloggers like Athol seem to be gifted enough to be married to completely submissive women and there is no one talking about how to maintain a successful marriage to a (feminist influenced) woman who rationally thinks she wants equality even though that's not how things play out all the time in the relationship."

Well yes and no. Jennifer is submissive, but it's not something that I made her be, she *is* submissive. She likes helping, serving, assisting, and caring yada yada yada. She doesn't like being micromanaged, but the reason she wants to be empowered and let loose is simply to do all the helping, serving, assisting and caring she wants to do. She likes the support role.

By way of comparison, back in the day I passed on dating a particular feminist friend that I was interested in. Nice girl, smart, pretty just with this huge feminist chip on her shoulder that I couldn't be bothered with. I just slowly found it a turn off and never pursued her. As far as I could tell in our little Christian circle of friends she never ended up dating anyone, so if her goal was not to be taken advantage of by men - mission accomplished.

So if I have any particular genius in managing submission, it's that I actually chose a submissive woman to marry. Really that's about 80% of everything right there though to be honest I did all that unwittingly. The problem I had was that by nature I am neither submissive nor dominant, but very highly self directed and introverted. This gives me the appearance of me being submissive in a LTR. I'm not seeking dominance naturally, so my partners tend to end up taking the dominant role. In some cases, this pisses them off and pisses me off that I'm not allowed to be self-directed.

In Jennifer's case she was so naturally submissive that she didn't take control over things, but we'd end up in sort of mutual submission deadlocks. "What do you want to do?" "I don't know what do you want to do?"

All that happened was that after many years together I kind of woke up to the dynamic that was happening. Plus as I got greater self assurance as I aged, I became more interested in asserting myself on the world and becoming more dominant in my interactions with other people.

How that plays out between us now is pretty low key. Most people that know us don't peg us as having some sort of dominant / submissive relationship; it's all pretty private and intimate. Well apart from the public blog and publishing of the whole book thing, but I'm just saying that if you're expecting her to be wearing a collar and sitting at my feet naked...

...oh hang on that's actually kinda hot.

Sorry wandered off a little there. Um... yeah... oh okay, I just started experimenting with being more assertive towards her and she lapped it up. Now it's really as much of a game between us as anything. I find simple tricks like planning dates or sexual positions just simple moves that work reliably and with minimal effort. She also says she doesn't like being teased, but she very much responds to me drawing playful attention to her positive response when I am dominant sexually. Plus it really doesn't hurt that I am a foot taller and outweigh her by 50%, there's just a natural vibe that comes from that dynamic without even hinting at potential violence.

The point is that I'm not trying to make her submissive, she is naturally submissive. On one hand I'm just letting it happen by not stopping her playing the support role and on the other I'm creating opportunities for her to play it. My lordly discipline over her is usually just saying "Thank you" when she does something nice for me. I am more proactive about giving her the sort of sex she likes more frequently, which tends towards being firmer than I naturally lean to... though I am gaining a taste for that.

Plus she's competent, as in really really competent. I have no clue how I'd live without her.

27 - Foreign Women Make The Best Wives?

August 14, 2010

I've read a number of places on game blogs about the idea of simply bypassing marrying an American woman due to their sexual hang ups / sluttiness / gold digging / sense of entitlement and marry a foreign woman from a more traditional culture.

I've had some minor experience with this.

Back in the good old days of evangelical Christianity I did a short term mission stint in Fiji. Not the touristy Fijian island, but the more heavily populated with ethnically Indian island of Fiji. That's Indian as in Indian's transported from India as workers/slaves courtesy of ye olde British Empire. Periodically the Indian group gets the short end of the stick from the more properly Fijian group and while I was there the stick was getting rattled loudly. A few months after I left, the military coup went down and the stick came out properly.

Anyway... here's how a typical attempt at me buying something in a store went...

Me: "Hi I'd like to buy a Coke."

Cashier: "Please have a free one."

Me: "Wow, so nice, thanks."

Cashier: "Now you must come home and have dinner with my family."

Me: "Ummm what?"

Cashier: "blah blah blah something in Hindi blah blah blah."

Then suddenly two or three other guys would show up from apparently the next store joining this one and be extremely friendly and happy to see me, and be very insistent that yes I just had to come home for dinner and meet the family. They just wanted to show hospitality....

So no matter the time of day, nine in the morning, two in the afternoon, eight at night, I'd be near kidnapped to these people's home and a meal would be prepared. Speaking kindly, these were people of modest means. I always had a sense that this was a better meal that they usually ate, though nothing much more than rice, chicken and some sort of spice.

Then the questions would start up, do I have a girlfriend, am I married yada yada yada. And there always was a girl, no doubt the prettiest one of whatever daughters of marriageable age there were in the family. They were always beautiful, polite, charming, well dressed and more often than not the one serving me the food. Then they were just staying attentive and leaning in close to hear better as the sudden rains pounded against the corrugated iron roof. Sitting as close as possible without touching.

I can't claim I had anything special about me. This was happening to all the guys I went with pretty much. I had three of these kidnapped-home-for-dinner events on the second day I was there. I never got a straight up marriage proposal, but it was absolutely clear that if I had wanted to leave with a beautiful submissive eighteen year old virgin it would have happened with a bidding frenzy like an eBay auction closing on Brittany Spears unwashed thongs.

But it was all a terrible trap. All they really wanted was a citizenship bridge out of Fiji. Once I had married the girl we would have lived in New Zealand. Then there would have been an endless stream of siblings, uncles, and cousins all using me and my house as the stepping stone to living in New Zealand too, with no way to realistically deny them indefinitely living with me until they found their footing. Just imagine the "family card" getting played on me from dawn to dusk by every relative she has. Usually the demand is sending money home to the wife's parents, but in this case the expectation would be some light money laundering to get assets out of Fiji. I'm 100% serious, these were desperate times for them.

So I passed on them all. After about a week I started reading the whole situation better and started politely declining the dinners at home routine. Word got around and things calmed down. Just the Coke please.

And for the record, some of those girls - not the ones with secret boyfriends (lol!) - were genuinely hopeful. A New Zealand passport created vagina tingle like a quarter million dollars. Despite knowing it was going to be a trap, when I left Fiji I had a real sense of unease about not saving one of them. Like I found a box of kittens and just kept walking.

28 - Sexy Move: Rescue Her

August 19, 2010

(Edit: This is when we were on vacation in New Zealand saying goodbye to Dad.)

Jennifer and the girls were out walking and the weather decided to mix it up with some heavy rain. They had their coats etc, but walking in heavy rain isn't much fun and we're without cell phones here.

So I circled the neighborhood in Dad's car looking for them. Found them in about five minutes at a park, the girls semi-drenched and happy, Jennifer slunk back against the shelter of the small building by the park. She hates being cold. Just hates it. She was very pleased to see me.

Eldest Daughter: "I didn't know we were in need of serious rescue."

Me: "You weren't."

But there were no complaints from anyone about a warm car and a fast shuttle home.

In general rescuing women from their own folly isn't a good idea, that can establish that your role is to be their personal safety net butler and encourage further folly, but rescuing them from random circumstance on your terms can earn a lot of points.

So anyway, rescue from some heavy rain by borrowed car isn't as dramatic as Arnold Schwarzenegger growling "If you want to live follow me", and cocking a pump action shotgun, but then who needs that sort of drama on vacation anyway.

29 - Male Mid-Life Crisis Is A Myth

August 20, 2010

The male mid-life crisis isn't what you think it is...it's about how old the man's wife is. A forty year old man with a forty year old wife has a mid-life crisis, a forty year old man with a twenty-five year old wife doesn't. A twenty-five year old man with a forty year old wife has a "mid-life crisis." It's really not about his age, it's about his partner moving into a non- or markedly less fertile phase of life, and his Body Agenda deciding to search for someone else that is more fertile. It's best to think of it as a "partner not so fertile crisis."

What happens when you have a "partner not so fertile crisis" is that your own body starts up a set of programming called "The Rationalization Hamster." The Hamster just goes into overdrive trying to drum up reasons to be pissed off at your spouse, ways to look on them negatively, ways to blow up minor issues into larger ones and generally any excuse to justify running off with a new partner or getting some on the sly.

The current partner may be doing nothing overtly wrong other than simply being less fertile and sexy.

On a hard wired level the Body Agenda impulse is going to drive your impulses towards finding another mate. Essentially all the Body Agenda cares about is whether or not you have an adequate food supply and can probably attract a younger vagina when it decides whether not to unleash the Rationalization Hamster. The Body Agenda knows nothing of divorce laws, child support, the 401k or how hard it is to get full market value from your house when you have to sell quickly. Frankly, the Rationalization Hamster is pretty irrational when it comes to that sort of thing. It's really more like one of those Disney personal shoulder devils.

So anyway have a think about that and whether or not you are tearing apart your own relationship with bullshit from the Rationalization Hamster if your wife is mid-30s to early 40s. Your wife may have been doing just fine and been ideal as a wife and your best friend. But the Body Agenda doesn't care about any of that, it just thinks there's enough food for another baby to be fed.

This is why seemingly smart men can self-destruct themselves half-way through life. After everything goes down, even if it goes fairly smoothly, many men can ultimately regret leaving their wife for a younger woman. Often the only thing the younger woman has over the wife is that she is younger, so there can be a sick moment of realization that your wife was a better woman and that you were actually happier with her. Having assloads of money aside... when you are 40-something you just aren't going to get the same level of quality of woman interested in you as when you were a 20-something.

For the ladies reading wondering what to do about their "mid-life crisis" husbands... You get yourself in the best shape you can and you turn up the sexy. Basically you mimic the behavior and appearance of a younger more fertile woman as best you can without looking like a try hard. And try not to get drawn into stupid fights with his Rationalization Hamster. That just makes it stronger, louder and more idiotic. And to be completely blunt now not is not the time you should be demanding that he love you just the way you are because you are a precious snowflake. That just underlines that you aren't what you used to be and intensifies the problem.

Tomorrow... women's end-of-fertility crisis...

30 - Female Mid-Life Crisis Is A Myth

August 20, 2010

I talked yesterday about the male version "mid-life crisis" actually being a "partner not so fertile crisis", today we'll hit on the female version. Naturally because men can continue to impregnate a woman for their entire lifespan barring medical difficulties, the female "mid-life crisis" is actually a crisis related to the end of her own fertility, but his age does play a role.

Both the husband and the wife can have these events happen in a perfect storm of both happening together, but I think for the most part one side of the relationship happens stronger than the other. I suspect it's usually the partner with the higher Sex Rank that gets the pleasure of struggling through this and inflicting it on the other partner. Once the partner with the higher Sex Rank starts having their little psychodrama, the lower ranked partner usually focuses on maintaining themselves in the relationship.

Also this isn't a menopause thing - that happens late 40s to early 50s- what I'm talking about happens earlier, when the wife is mid 30s to early 40s. As far as your Body Agenda cares, female fertility is all but gone by mid 30s, menopause is in many ways just a statement of how well the modern food supply and medical care keeps us alive for so long. For the majority of human history, 99% of women wouldn't have reached menopause anyway. I don't mean to make menopause seem trivial to live through, just underlining that it isn't what I'm talking about.

What happens to a wife having her fertility crisis is basically the same thing a single childless woman goes through in her early to mid 30s. It's that all purpose generalized panic to find a partner to father a child with her. For a single woman it's typically a need to get any children made, for a married woman it's usually a need to get "one more" made before the shot clock runs down on the expiration date of her eggs. And like I said yesterday as long as there is a food supply, most women's Body Agendas vote for having babies... even if she would on an intellectual level rather be selected for a Space Shuttle mission, complete a second doctorate or whatever awesome thing that women can do these days. Or perhaps she'd rather just not have to blow up like a zeppelin again and change diapers for another two years... just as the current crop of kids can finally get themselves to and from school and can help around the house.

As both men and women age, we become less sexually appealing on a genetic level to mate with. I'm currently 40 and have better resources, presence and sexual technique than when I was 20. Given the choice between me at 40 or me at 20 raising her kids, Jennifer is going to much prefer me at 40. However if she gets the baby making crazies a shot of semen from me at 20 is going to sound like a much better idea to her Body Agenda than getting one from me at 40. It's the same DNA I'd be passing on to her, it's just that it's not quite so fresh (aka Alpha) as what I'd be blasting into her twenty years ago. So cue up her Rationalization Hamster to complain about the position of the toilet seat being a statement of how I'm not committed to the marriage and am purposely seeking to offend her. (Not that this happened or anything, I keep the toilet seat firmly down because if I don't it makes my mother back in New Zealand angry.)

What happens for wives having their end of fertility crisis is basically one of two possible outcomes. The first is that nothing much happens overtly because her husband has enough of an Alpha profile with emphasis on physical health and vigor that her Body Agenda votes for hubby as an acceptable mate. She just becomes a bit more sexually willing and horny with her husband. This actually is awesome for the husband and not really much of a crisis to struggle with. Thumbs up, bring it on!

The other general outcome is that if her Body Agenda decides hubby doesn't have the best profile for getting her pregnant, then the Rationalization Hamster kicks in full force. The resulting fitness test doesn't just happen over one day or one event like a chick in a bar asking for you to buy her a drink, it just cranks up into a endless hurricane of testing that can last years or until the dramatic conclusion of the relationship. Divorce is possible, her cheating is possible, "I need space", "I love you but I'm not in love with you", "What the hell is wrong with you? I have told you and told you about where to put the plates and bowls in the dishwasher. The PLATES GO THERE AND THE #$%^ING BOWLS GO THERE." Basically overly Beta husbands get their shit kicked in. God help you if you squeeze the toothpaste from the wrong end.

And again, this is all Body Agenda stuff. The wife may not want more kids for plenty of logical reasons, it's just an internal conflict between two different impulses.

I think I've spelled out along the way what the husband needs to do to handle his wife having this sort of crisis. It's really just what I've been saying all along on the blog. Get into physical shape, balance the Alpha and Beta stuff... and make sure you enjoy the ride.

31 - Only Boys Have Mojo

August 30, 2010

(Edit: We had just flown back to America)

My body is on New Zealand Time, my head is on Eastern Standard Time and my stomach has gotten stuck on Lunch Time.

Anyway, a quick email conversation from Friday...

Me: (something work related)... and I'm starting to feel like I'm getting my mojo back.

She: (something work related)... ah, me = no mojo

Me: Well of course you have no mojo, you're a girl. Only boys have mojo.

She: So what do girls have?

Entire Weekend Passes As I Live Like Newly Transported Nocturnal Zoo Animal And Monday Rolls Around

Me: Kryptonite

She: LMAO.

I'm hungry again...

32 - Resistance Is Futile

September 3, 2010

(Edit: The image that went with this post was a picture of Pikachu with the caption, "Your resistance only makes my penis harder!" Which is probably disturbing on several levels...)

Apparently my blog is great, but I'm....

A traitor for not championing Men's Rights.
Hateful towards women.
An idiot for being married.
Heartless for being pro-divorce.
Leading men to their doom for being pro-marriage.
Reducing everything to tits and ass.
Brilliant for pointing out the obvious nature of men's interest in tits and ass.
Not writing enough for women.
Not explaining things enough.
Writing too much about sex.
Going to get raped in divorce court when Jennifer goes dark side on me.
A bad parent.
A loser trying to convince myself that I'm a winner.
Soulless and don't understand love.
Have a touching romance with my wife.
Need to take a spiritual view of things.
Shallow.
Not the sort of man you'd want to marry.
Have ridiculously high standards for choosing a wife.
Don't know anything about game because Jennifer is an easy wife.
Have no game because I'm married.
Think game solves everything in marriage.

A natural Alpha.
A total Beta.

So yeah... I have no clue how to address all this.
I just think I'm the underdog that got the girl. I'm going to keep talking and posting as long as people listen.

And a big thanks to all those do say encouraging things and make constructive comments. It really does make a difference to me.

As an aside... compliments also make my penis harder too. It's a vicious cycle.

33 - Samuel Adams: Not Always A Good Decision

September 5, 2010

I don't drink very much... about 1-2 drinks a week. Plus I never got into the real boozing scene at college being at the time a fairly squeaky clean Christian guy. As such my alcohol tolerance is fairly low and thanks to an experiment that I run maybe once every 4-5 years I've established that six drinks is going to have me cuddling up to a toilet bowl with a deep personal sense of regret.

Here's how it plays out for me drinking...

One drink actually gets me a moderate buzz, but I'm still very much in control of myself with one drink.

Two drinks gets me a full on buzz and that slight sense of loss of perfect coordination. I probably seem like I'm walking fine, but I can feel that I'm not. I also become quite touchy feely in a huggy, arm around your waist, stroke your arm sort of way...

However at three drinks I've basically lost control. Touchy feely turns into increasingly brazen impulsivity. At some point I come to the very firm decision that I am going to have sex with someone. Someone in this room. Hi there, wow this place is like Vagina World suddenly.

Four and five drinksh kinda merge into one, because I've already had three drinksh, which is the gateway drink to four drinksh and four drinksh is kinda like that math networking thing where two plus two equals five because of the synrgy, the sineggy, the signegry... the way the drinksh work together ash a team. I want to fuck you. Your breasts are nicesh.

Six drinksh and we're gonna just go schomewhere and... BBBBRRRRRROOOOOOGGGGGHHHHHFFFF!!!

So anyway... somewhere along the way I decided that I only drink with Jennifer around. It's not her rule, it's mine. I've never actually done anything particularly stupid with someone else while drinking because I hardly ever drink, and the times I have Jennifer has been around. Also at 3+ drinks I'm so studfucking overconfident I can get her in the sack that she just becomes the easy mark anyway. Her main concern by this point is that it doesn't happen in a public place or break furniture.

There have been a couple of exceptions of course when I have had something to drink without Jennifer, all of them work related. Each time I let know Jennifer where I'm going, who I'm with and my expected time of return. Honestly she trusts me more than I trust myself. Like I said, these are my rules for me. That being said it really does help me stay well behaved. If she asked me to come home I would.

My natural high sexual interest + alcohol + added confidence with women in the last few years, just all seems a bit much to handle at once. I can handle 2 out of the 3 no problem, but it would be just outstandingly stupid to tear a hole into everything we have together over having a few Samuel Adams...

34 - The Rhododendrons Of Unusual Size

September 6, 2010

I'm not a huge yard work fan. Yet in the last few days I have mowed the lawn, trimmed the shrubs back, and done the majority of the grunt work of hacking down the Rhododendrons Of Unusual Size (ROUS) that blocked out the view of the street from the 1st floor of the house.

Actually we're in a split level so perhaps we're on the 0.5st floor or the 1.5st floor, I'm not really sure which. Anyway, we're quite high up and the ROUS were blocking the view of the street. Youngest is now in middle school and waits for the school bus across the road, down the street, around the corner but still in direct line of sight of our living room window. Except the ROUS totally blocks the view, so it's kind of more like pine of sight than anything.

Jennifer didn't particularly complain about the ROUS, but I understood that she needs the ability to stand sentinel-like in the living room each morning and look out at youngest. Eldest is with youngest, so nothing is likely to happen anyway so I have no great concerns about them. Plus they purposely stand behind a tree on the neighbors property so as avoid line of sight from our house. So really the purpose of taking down the ROUS is to get a better view of a tree about 50 yards away. But like I said, I know Jennifer needs to be able to see that tree that the kids hide behind waiting for the school bus.

So down it all has to come. My original idea was just to wrap a rope around the base of it and tie it to the trailer-hitch of my car and try and drive off with it. Then I realized that was a completely stupid idea. I mean Jennifer has a car as well, so there really was no point risking mine with my shenanigans. I had mentioned this to her yesterday and she respectfully disagreed with me on this plan. It's always good to talk in a marriage.

So at 4:30am I got up and went to sneak outside and put the plan into action, but she was up checking on the kid that had somehow migrated to sleeping in the living room on the couch. So I quickly recovered and earned valuable marriage points by offering to stand watch as male protector and shooed Jennifer back to bed. Nevertheless the sleeping child on a couch against the wall of the house that supported the weight of the ROUS was a sufficient deterrent to execution of my plan.

So I went to Plan B. I slept until the crack of noon and stumbled dazed and confused into the kitchen for coffee. I like my coffee like my women - I want them to wake me up in the morning and kick start my day. Then it's outside in the special gardening attire - also known as what I wore yesterday - and armed with only a standard saw, raw masculine energy and ignorance, I set about the felling of the ROUS.

The first phase was as glamorous as a model falling off the catwalk as I crawled on my belly into the heart of the ROUS. Once inside I was struck by the majesty of the thing and the spaciousness of the massive plant. There was shelter from the elements, a cushioned natural floor from the leaves, and a sense of privacy and yet the exhibitionist thrill of being outside. It was the perfect porn fortress.

Now with a twinge of regret I started on the multitude of branches and limbs. I'll save you the details of the sawing and the dragging and the chopping. Suffice to say that the sentence you read just prior covered about two hours of the aforementioned sawing and dragging and chopping of the ROUS. At some point during the effort I bounced the saw off my left thumb and had a single saw tooth bite through about six of the seven layers of skin. I count myself lucky to tell the tale.

With the ROUS gone, the secondary ROUS looked stupid by itself, though it didn't actually block the view of the tree that the girls hide behind waiting for the bus. Reported wifely complaint "it doesn't look balanced now" and I had to agree in my own dominant masculine way that it did not. Commence another hour of sawing and dragging and chopping.

In Jennifer's defense, and seeing she's my editor I better give her one, she was there the whole time chopping and dragging and raking too. So after about three hours of work, both ROUS were down and somewhat inelegantly piled against the side of the house facing the neighbors we don't like. Then we all went inside and washed off the muck and Jennifer cooked us all breakfast, or lunch, or whatever it's called when your wife finally feeds you something to eat at three o'clock in the afternoon. Maybe the word I'm looking for is neglect.

Anyway, the ROUS might have really started getting under her skin if left too long and yes I'm teasing her just a little about the kids hiding behind the tree. It's not a shit test to clear the ROUS, it's a reasonable request and one that Jennifer couldn't complete nearly as well as I could. I hate yard work, but I'm glad we got it all done together.

So good job everyone. The living room looks vastly brighter now and that's a good thing. Task completion is always good as well and now that she gets a better view of the tree that the kids hide behind in the morning, I'm expecting at least a 25% increase in the strength of her orgasms.

35 - Sexy Move: Dirty Talk

September 15, 2010

Most women enjoy dirty talk in bed. Often this is limited to the bedroom and not an all area pass. I.e. calling her a "hot little slut" as you are all hot, sweaty and flinging the covers off the top of you and on to the floor is sexy goodness. Calling her a "hot little slut" in the checkout line at the supermarket is another. Proper etiquette when standing in line is to not say that sort of thing at all, but to text it.

If you struggle to come up with dirty things to say, just talk about what is happening. Short positive statements, "yeah suck me like that," work well.

Tell her to do something, if only a position change. "On your back now." (Don't say "please")

Announce your impending orgasm... "almost there baby, stay right there."

Sometimes you don't even need to say anything... just breathe a little harder near her ear so she can hear it.

36 - Sexy Move: Hit The Big Red Easy Button

September 16, 2010

In one of the comments yesterday...

"I too, love dirty talk! I have flat out told my husband exactly what to say. His response: I can't call you that! I love you! ...doesn't get it (sigh!) Men are inhibited in this area; I blame the Madonna-Whore complex."

When your wife tells you she is into something sexually, she's pretty much handing you a big red "easy" button to push to make her very, very wet and very, very happy.

Option One....
Her: "Having my hair pulled turns me on."
You: (pulls her hair)
Her: "Uuuuuuuuhhhhhhhhh!!!!! Oh yeah...OMG fuck me!"

Option Two...
Her: "Having my hair pulled turns me on."
You: "I don't want to hurt you though"
Her: "Ummmm. Yeahhh... okay, fuck off."

See if you refuse to push that button for her, whatever that button is, that's going to really, really frustrate her. Plus if she's talking and telling you she's into certain things, she's probably on the horny end of the scale as well.

Try for a moment and think what bad things might happen to you when you purposely by omission sexually frustrate a horny woman.

So when she says... Pull my hair. Spank me. Call me a slut. Do that harder. A little higher up and don't stop.... is it really that hard to pay attention? Hit the easy button. Hit it hard. Hit it with your dick.

37 - Sexy Move: Make The Bed Squeak

September 18, 2010

A few days ago I mentioned that most women like dirty talk in bed. Adding on to that, they just like bedroom noise in general. She wants to believe that you're totally into her and breathless and out of control with lust for her.

One very simple tactic to make her think she's being completely pounded into a pool of her own juices, is to find the right rhythm that makes the bed squeak. We have a pretty sturdy King Size wooden framed thing that took an awful lot of effort to get into the house and put together. It's really solid. However when I'm on top of Jennifer there is a level of my movement that is just right to make it start oscillating just a little and the whole thing starts making a five decibels above discreet squeaking noise. It's kind of the same principle that high winds can rip a badly designed bridge apart by getting it slowly wobbling more and more. (See, this is why you should have paid more attention in physics class.)

It's really not anything hugely rough that's going on, it's firm to be sure, but it's not even as rough as it could be. It's about 87.3% of maximum roughness. It just sounds like she's getting the shit fucked out of her. If you were standing outside our bedroom door you'd be touching yourself.

Bonus points if you can bang the headboard against the wall. That's like hotel sex. Women love hotel sex. Half the reason women have affairs is just to be in a hotel I think. They will say that's because it's romantic... "Romantic" being the girl talk word for "costs money."

Pro Tip: Some beds can be made squeakier by the use of a screwdriver and the loosening of a few screws. No one ever got divorced because they broke the bed by fucking. However I am not buying you a new bed.

Warning: Make sure the banging sound is not her head against the headboard. Women detest that.

38 - Don't Move Out Just Because She Told You To

September 24, 2010

Following on from yesterday where the scenario is (1) she wants you out, and (2) there is no other man in the picture - which is NOT a guarantee just because she has stated no one else is involved - and (3) the cause of the problem is largely your lack of attention at holding up your end of the deal in the relationship.

I've realized I missed mentioning one of the most important things NOT to do, in part because the reader I had been emailing had done it correctly. I also had a couple emails addressing it as well. (Thank you to those who did so.)

The most important thing to NOT do is leave when she asks you to. Just utterly refuse to go. If you just put your tail between your legs and slink away because she told you to, you have just completely framed her as the dominant / Alpha of the relationship. It's all but impossible to regain that frame and it will markedly reduce her interest in you even further. This is in essence nothing more than a very, very serious shit test.

The same with sleeping on the couch. Just don't go. Same reasons as above.

The correct frame is "if you want to break up this family without even trying, you're the one walking out the door."

Also important is that by leaving the family home you are setting the stage for the future, where should divorce happen you've established that (1) you left and (2) she's performed 99% of all the child care and has possession of the house. Even assuming a magical 100% perfectly fair family court, possession is nine tenths of the law and the court will likely just roll with the current set up and some visitation and child support siphoning for you.

Also once you are out of the house, all she has to do is change the locks and you can't even gain access to your own house without some sort of major incident. If the cops arrive as you're banging on the front door and yelling at your wife to open up, you're toast.

Plus if you were wrong about the "no one else involved" thing and you move out, the secret boyfriend can move right in, or just have a far easier time of finding a comfy bed to have sex with her in. Plus he can just take your lawn mower if she lets him.

If you're moved out, you have minimal ability to effect a positive change on the relationship by incidental moments of interaction together. Mostly you're just giving her time to adapt to you not being there, and after a while her mood will return to its baseline normal happiness and she'll believe that's she's happier without you.

Any and all of this can go down before she's even filed for a divorce.

This may of course turn into a very difficult discussion when she tells you leave and you refuse to go. Normally I'd expect some increased screaming and verbal threats. This you continue to verbalize understanding that yes indeed things are very bad right now and you are willing to work with her on changing things, but you do not agree to leaving or quit the relationship.

What I'm suggesting here is a form of passive resistance aka Gandhi / Martin Luther King / Boston Tea Party where you simply refuse to take part in implementing your own oppression. It really shouldn't lead to violence on her part, but should things escalate beyond merely verbal, you may have to get police involvement. If so, make absolutely sure that you are the one that calls not her. Call 911 and follow their instructions. Even using force in self-defense can come back to haunt you. There's no perfect solution at this level of conflict.

39 - Her Orgasm, Or Not Her Orgasm... What Was The Question?

October 9, 2010

The Alpha approach is to simply not give a damn about her orgasm or sexual pleasure. It's simply about getting her to do want you want her to do to maximize your pleasure.

The Beta approach is to do whatever it takes to make her orgasm and be sexually pleased.

With the Alpha approach you can sometimes get into that eyes glazed over zone where the fact that you're married is of no consequence. You're just banging a chick. She just happens to be your wife.

With the Beta approach you can get real pleasure from her pleasure. It can be its own little power trip that you made her orgasm.

Lacking one or the other approaches ultimately becomes a turn off for her. All Alpha all the time and after a while she starts wondering when it's ever going to be her turn. All Beta all the time and she starts feeling like the bed is a stage and she has to perform for you.

So as always, the solution is if you're too Alpha and add Beta and if you're too Beta add Alpha. It's also not always possible to really hit both angles in a single sexual session, so don't worry about that. It's about the generalized balance over the long term.

But seeing the majority of readers likely live too much towards the Beta end of the scale... don't neglect just treating her like a piece of ass once in a while. If she says she's too tired or whatever, but it's not really much of a strong no, try telling her "well I only need you for five minutes, so why don't you go get ready." Hold the eye contact and use that naughty boy smile.

If she agrees, then only make it last five minutes. Thank her and do a long deep kiss... then go do something else.

40 - She's A Bad Bad Girl (Sometimes)

October 10, 2010

If she is interested in any of the more freaky stuff, she'll likely eventually seek it out. If you don't make yourself an option for exploring that aspect of herself with, things might eventually get... *awkward.*

Particularly with marrying a sexually inexperienced "good girl" you need to be open to the possibility of change. Ten years into a marriage, a 34 year old is going to feel far more confident of what is going on than the 24 year old she was. If you scrunch her into the "good girl" mantle forevermore, she may start seeing you as the jailer of her sexuality. If she decides to plot some little escapes you'll be the last to know.

Half the reason women like the bad boys so much is that they get to play the role of bad girl.

41 - The Second Date Rule

October 12, 2010

Assuming your wife displays some sort of highly negative behavior (read as "cray-zee biatch"), a good rule of thumb is The Second Date Rule...

If what she just did happened on the second date, would there have been a third date?

If the answer is "no", it's probably best to say something about it and not just suck it up for the rest of your marriage. The behavior will likely continue without it being addressed.

Women do respond positively to men who are not willing to put up with them being venomous screechtards. Both in general relationship terms and sexual terms. Just not at first.

42 - Janet Loves Fred: How Much Fatter Does Janet Get?

October 14, 2010

Math Problem: Janet meets Fred and they start a committed relationship together. Assume that the sex is good and she is into Fred. In the first year of the relationship how much fatter does Janet get? Show your work and explain why.

Answer: Janet's Body Agenda strategizes for a potential pregnancy, and runs the additional hunger subroutine supported by positive mood increase neurotransmitters and authorizes The Rationalization Hamster to advocate for dessert. The Body Agenda purposefully builds up an additional supply of body fat to better support the development of an unborn child should food shortages occur while pregnant.

Over the last six months of pregnancy, a woman needs an additional 300 calories a day.

So... 300 calories x 30 days x 6 months = 54000 calories

There are 3500 calories in a pound of human body fat.

So... 54000 calories divided by 3500 = 15.4 pounds

Rounding down 15.4 pounds ~ 15 pounds

Because Janet is into Fred, Janet gets 15 pounds heavier.

Disclaimer: Married Man Sex Life does not advocate getting ready for triplets real or imagined in this manner. Fifteen extra pounds is a little more boom in the booty and sexy, forty-five extra pounds is a medical issue.

43 - Say You're Sorry And Put It Right

October 20, 2010

Upon occasion you are going to totally screw something up and be in the wrong. I'm not talking "gee I'm failing a shit test" wrong, I'm talking, objectively, provably wrong. Why did you do that wrong. Where are the kids wrong. You taped over the wedding video wrong. Idiot, now we need to go to the ER wrong.

The solution is simple.

Say you're sorry and put right whatever can be put right.

It's amazing how often situations can be defused by a simple admission of wrongdoing and failure. Often what drives people's anger higher and higher is the wrongdoer's resistance to admitting obvious wrongdoing.

But sometimes that just doesn't seem to be enough. Sometimes that story about what you did comes back around and around and no amount of apologies seem to make a dent in the situation. Plus you put right whatever you could put right long ago.

After a while the actual current problem stops being the original incident and starts being the unforgiving rage of the original victim. So they are the ones that have to fix that problem. So at some point you have to say you can't apologize anymore as they are actively choosing to refuse to accept it. They actively want to remain angry. The problem lies on their end, not yours. Say so.

Just bear in mind that the worse the original incident, the longer you should allow for the anger process to work through. There's some difference between forgetting her birthday and the time you were goofing off and accidentally shot her in the ass with the nail gun.

44 - The Charity Event That Cannot Be Spoken Of

October 22, 2010

I can't tell you exactly what Jennifer and I are doing tonight, all I can say is that we are at "The Charity Event That Cannot Be Spoken Of." See if I tell you where exactly we are going, because my web presence is so much stronger than TCETCBSO, every time someone searches online for TCETCBSO, this blog would show up as the #1 search result. Seeing TCETCBSO is work related for both of us, that might be... awkward.

This annual event is in its 9th year and Jennifer, despite complaining loudly that she dislikes the work for TCETCBSO, takes an ever increasing role in the production of it. This year she is essentially one of two primary organizers. Naturally she does not complain at work... she complains to me.

There's a long tedious process of creating the TCETCBSO that starts six months before the event, then the event itself, then about a month of Monday morning quarterbacking. So about seven months a year the TCETCBSO is a topic of conversation and we're in the 9th year of this thing.

As I've made clear I pretty much started off heavy on the Beta end of the scale and I am too nice for the most part. So for about the first six run throughs of this event I listened to Jennifer and engaged in polite conversations about TCETCBSO while my rage slowly began to boil.

At some point in year 7 I just said fucking enough bi-atch and set up some limits;

I will attend the event.
I will help set up the event.
I will help out during the event.
Jennifer has to wear something that makes her look particularly sexy to the event.
I'm not selling tickets to the event.
I'm not finding items for the silent auction.
I'm not listening to you anymore about TCETCBSO.
La la la la la la la la la la I'm not listening la la la la.

Overall my new plan has worked extremely well the last three years. I'm having far more of a sense of humor about the whole thing. Plus work people knowing that we have an ongoing "marital spat" over TCETCBSO seems to act as an all purpose defense against further involvement with TCETCBSO. This comes in very handy considering my direct supervisor is the other primary organizer.

Of course people keep trying to sell me tickets to it. I think it's just to hear me tell them that I buy the ticket off someone that's having sex with me, thanks for nothing. Actually that must be a thing that's going around because someone threatened Jennifer yesterday that they were going to sell me a ticket. To their shock Jennifer informed them that I was buying one from her because she's the one fucking me. She just looks like Goldilocks... she'll cut you bitch, she'll cut you.

45 - Me So Hordey

November 5, 2010

Jennifer's old college roommate was staying over with us last night and we went out for breakfast this morning. We were walking into the local diner and, reaching the door first, I held the door open and Jennifer and her roomie walked in ahead of me. As we waited for the waitress to come over and seat us, there was some guy in a mechanics shirt also hovering near the reception area. Jennifer was completely unaware of him, but he very clearly looked her over and must have decided that her breasts were her best feature because his gaze returned to languish on them for several seconds...

... then he noticed me, noticing him, noticing her.

I'm tall more than I am big, honestly I could trim off a few pounds still so I don't really feel thuggish either. But today I just happened to be so cool I was rocking a long sleeved shirt under a short sleeved shirt. And my short sleeved shirt was a dried blood looking World of Warcraft Horde faction symbol on a dirty brown background. It's very tribal looking. It's the sort of shirt that says "I don't care what sex you are, you will have a vagina when I'm done with you."

So apparently today I'm scary looking as he clearly had a very obvious startle reaction when he made eye contact with me. The whole head snapping back, bug eyed and defensive arm position thing. He took a step in the direction of away.

Expressionless, I rolled past him with two women.

46 - It's Not Your Job To Cure Their Sexual Dysfunction

November 8, 2010

Sometimes you meet someone and the connection is instant and special. But there's a problem. Your sex drive is clearly mismatched, or even worse they have serious sexual issues that impede the relationship advancing.

It's not your job in a dating relationship to cure their sexual dysfunction.

I had a serious relationship in college that honestly stayed at nothing more than a friendship level. She had a few issues going on and despite my enormous attraction I held back from dating her, but we hung out all the time. Studying in the library every day, lunch every day, coffee, church. I just waited for her to get a bit more together before pushing for the relationship I actually wanted. And I waited, and waited and waited...

One day we had started discussing sex, and the frequency of sexual impulse and horniness came up.

Me: "About five or six times"

She: "I dunno once or twice."

We just stood there looking at each other, waiting...

Me: "...a day."

She: "...a month."

Me: "Really?"

She: "Really."

Bearing in mind that this was back in my Evangelical Christian period, I never considered her again as a possible relationship. All done sorry, you are not the wife I am looking for. I've never really figured out if she just wasn't interested in me, or couldn't really be interested in anyone anyway. I just sure as hell wasn't wasting my one shot at sexual happiness on her. Later I met Jennifer and my friend was fairly useful as life support for me getting through the hell of long distance without Jennifer.

Actually looking back it was all very complicated. She was on the short list to be the If I Didn't Have Jennifer I Would Probably Have Somebody Else (edit: references a fabulous Tim Minchin song). My choice in wife was the right one, but I couldn't have made it to the end without her help. But if she had made a move on me I would have folded and failed. It's humbling. It was a hard lonely time and I have no taste for time apart from Jennifer.

So anyway... if you are romantically involved with someone with sexual issues, marrying them isn't a cure for it. All that happens is that you win a sexual problem too.

I have tried to look up my old friend a few times but I haven't found her. I hope she's ok. She may not be.

47 - Understanding And Reacting To The Female Arm Slap

November 9, 2010

I love the faux arm slap thing that women sometimes give me. It usually means that I have absolutely scored a direct hit in the vagina tingle department and it's a clear Indicator Of Interest (IOI).

My solution is not to hit them back with an arm slap, but to verbally draw further attention to their sexual interest in me. "Well obviously that excited you", "You can't help touching me I see", "Little miss spicy likes to play rough I see... I can go there." With Jennifer I just escalate physical touch and pull her in to me usually and kiss. If I slap back, it's always a little pat on the butt, but for the most part if you frame it as her IOI in you and play it off cocky and funny, you come out as playfully naughty and women lap that up.

I also suspect that the arm slap is an unconscious way of a woman assessing the man's muscle tone. If you notice they don't slap unattractive or badly unfit men that way. If they slap you and it's all squishy fat it's not so sexy, if they slap you and it's solid muscle it is sexy. It's an actual fitness test.

Also wincing in pain or recoiling from a slap is a huge weakness display and going to turn her interest in you down. Just take the slap and immediately roll the routine that she's expressing interest in you. Otherwise she's going to think you're the sort of guy that secretly wants a Hello Kitty tattoo.

48 - Jennifer Shuts Me Up

November 14, 2010

Jennifer: "I stole $20 from your wallet."

Me: "It's only stealing if we don't have sex."

Jennifer: "Well you owe me then."

Me: (Look of utter befuddlement)

Me: "I have no idea what that means."

Jennifer: "I have no idea either."

Me: "So... er.... ah."

VERBAL INTERACTION FAILURE OVERRIDE PROTOCOL INITIATED

EXECUTE PHYSICAL ESCALATION ROUTINE ALPHA-TEN SECOND KISS

TARGET COMPLIANT ALPHA-TEN SECOND KISS

REBOOT SPEECH MODULE

Me: "That's almost worth $20."

Jennifer: "Almost?!"

Me: "Maybe some more practice together...."

Jennifer: "You're incorrigible!"

INDICATOR OF INTEREST VERBAL-24 RECOGNIZED

SEXUAL ADVANCE PROTOCOL INITIATED

SCANNING FOR LIFE SIGNS

TWO CHILDREN PRESENT AT THIS LOCATION RANDOM DEPLOYMENT NOTED

TARGET UNABLE TO BE ISOLATED

STATE VERBAL INTENTION AND END PROTOCOL

Me: "I'll see some more of you later...."

STATUS DETERMINATION: HUNGRY

DEPLOY TO KITCHEN

As an aside, we have a joint checking account so it's all "our money" anyway. We're playing with each other.

49 - Dad: 1945-2010 (A Letter Of Reference)

November 19, 2010

Dad passed away peacefully this morning. There will be a gathering of some sort and New Zealand is simply too far to go to make it in time. As such I planned ahead and wrote this farewell piece several weeks back for when it was needed. He was still able to read it then and understand it.

Everything I wrote about my father is true. Only after I finished the piece did I realize that everything I had written was also about me. Or at least what I would like to be true about me. Much of the content of our lives is different, but the style is so much the same.

To Whom It May Concern.

Please allow me to introduce Warwick Kay. Warwick has been working in his chosen field for some 65 years, spending the last 40 of them in my employment. As he is undecided on his next career move, this letter of reference will have to remain general in tone. Suffice to say I firmly believe that in whatever capacity he is employed in the future, he will remain as well liked, productive and diligent as he has been with us these many years.

Warwick is a man of remarkable intelligence and thought. Despite a lack of formal higher education he has a way of finding a new approach to old problems that often solves them. Likewise while he is grounded in what is possible and is free of magical thinking, he is not afraid to dream up something big. Simply put, if Warwick says something can be done, despite the appearance of his idea being impossible to outsiders, he can actually follow through and do it.

Warwick is fiercely competitive. He will with dogged determination do whatever it takes to find a way to win, whether that takes a single try or the better part of a decade to break through to the pinnacle, he will keep hammering at it. Though he is competitive that zest for victory comes with a keen sense of fair play and what is right. Not only will he beat you within the rules, he sticks to the spirit of the rules' intention too.

Warwick has an excellent sense of humor and fun. His personal hygiene is adequate.

Warwick is also generous with his willingness to offer help when asked. He offers advice without seeking manipulation of the asker into somehow benefiting himself.

Warwick is a builder. Whether that be; a terraced garden where there was just a wicked sloping backyard, an International level Go-Kart track where there was a swamp, a top quality bed and breakfast where there was just a house, or a friendship where there were strangers, he always leaves where he has been placed better off for his passing through.

As minor counterpoints to this glowing report; occasionally boisterousness has resulted in uncalled for wear and tear to company vehicles, also his sick day use recently has been somewhat excessive.

Yours,

Athol Kay

Mum and Dad met on a blind date and were married 45 years. Dad tried his best to overcome the cancer and played a good defense for over two years. Mum nursed him at home until the end. She read this letter at the final gathering and I'm told the personal hygiene line got a huge laugh. Dad would have roared with laughter too.

50 - Sexy Move: Disco Is Female Kryptonite

November 29, 2010

Jennifer's parents have this amazing street that still goes all out for Halloween, so we make it into our annual Candy Mecca for the kids. Of course kids with cell phones and Facebook talk to other kids... and pretty soon the word on the street is that the Kay kids have the hot ticket and pretty soon we have the entire giggle of girls wanting in.

So knowing that I'm going to play taxi driver for my youngest daughter and her friends down to my in-laws place, I decide to plan ahead. Actually let me explain why I have to plan ahead. These are all good kids, but one of them is like Kermit the Frog on cocaine in terms of the sheer verbiage that spews from her mouth. She is a good kid, she's not disrespectful or anything, but it's just like Robin Williams and a Gatling gun made a baby together and she has the Gatling gun's sense of humor. I feel bad for just tolerating her, but I just can't take it.

So anyway... 30 minute car ride with this kid. Something has to be done.

I hatch a plan. I pop into Target and buy a cheap "Best of Disco" CD. Once the kids are piled into the car I pop the CD in and just play the disco at them at a moderate level and it's like freaking magic.

"Oh I love this song."
"OMG I know this one."
"Can you turn up the radio Mr. Kay?" (Yes. Yes I can.)

By the time we get down to the in-laws I have some totally tamed 6th Grade girls. They pile out of the car singing and dancing... "At the Car Wash! Whoa-ah-whoa-oh!" and doing the hip bump thing together. Jennifer driving the other car with more kids is just amazed at me.

"What did you do to them?"
"Oh nothing, just played some disco."
"Haha really?"
"Oh yeah, girls are easy for me."
Eye rolling and groaning, but a smile.
"Well you're easy for me aren't you?"
She slaps my arm.

Anyway we had a good time with Halloween and more disco on the way back home. You know, just to establish the operant conditioning. I didn't realize how much they enjoyed it until about a week ago when a couple of the kids are over visiting and doing something in the living room with my kids and I get home from work. I do the normal "hi kids" routine and plonk down at the computer. A few minutes later guess what I hear from them...

"At the Car Wash! Whoa-ah-whoa-oh!"

Holy crap. Disco is like kryptonite for girls and they associate seeing me with hearing it. Who knew? I think I'm going to do some field testing on women and see how it works out.

Update: In writing this post I was hunting up some YouTube disco and I instantly caught Jennifer singing and grooving along to... "Do a little dance, make a little love, get down tonight..."

51 - Sexy Move: Find Some Stolen Time Together

December 10, 2010

If Game can be summarized into three words, it's "Instigate, Isolate, and Escalate." The instigation being that sense of playful engaging interaction with her. Whether that's banter, teasing, deep and meaningful talking, humor or whatever, you're trying to start something with her beyond asking her what's for dinner.

Escalate being the "always be closing" approach of physical touch, sexual touch and lets go to the bedroom. I'm not saying every time you touch you are forcing the issue towards naked sexy time, just that you are setting the intent that there will be a sexy naked time and it's going to be good. If she wants sex, you can follow through on that.

Instigation and escalation are fairly easily done in a marriage. You can always talk and play together, and no one gets offended if a married couple play a little grab ass and kiss each other. But the harder one to get done is isolation if you have a couple of little cockblocks roaming your house asking for things to eat and allowance.

So you need to find ways to get rid of the kids or manage to shake them off. Everyone talks about weekly Date Nights like they are the Holy Grail of a good marriage, but honestly they can be fairly expensive to do routinely. I think Jennifer and I have done 3 or 4 of them this year.

What we do though is try and find sneaky ways of alone time together. Our kids are old enough to be home alone so Jennifer and I often do grocery shopping together. That seems kind of dull I know, but we're together without the kids and just get to hang out like the old times. Plus we can plan the meals we're cooking together during the week. I get to do the heavy lifting and stuff like that. We both like it.

Also shopping only really takes about an hour and we're usually gone for about an hour and a half. There's a Panera Bread next to the grocery store and we have coffee and a medium fancy snack / lunch of some sort together and just talk.

The kids have no clue that we actually escaped them and had fun.

52 - My Husband Is Scared Of Me

December 12, 2010

I had a short conversation a few days back that has stuck with me. I was asked point blank "who makes the decisions in your marriage?" by a fairly newly married woman I know vaguely, but who also knows Jennifer reasonably well. I've never been asked this question directly by a person in real life and I was struck by how very personal of a question it was. Answering it truthfully had a slight sense of "outing" us...

."..so who makes the decisions in your marriage?"

"I do."

"Really?!"

"Yes. We talk a lot about things but ultimately I make final decisions on things if we need one. It's fairly mutual but there's a 51/50 balance of power there too."

Then she surprised me...

"I make the decisions. My husband is scared of me."

Damn. That. Just. Happened.

Holy cow, I couldn't imagine being in a relationship with a woman that scared me. I'm happy to frame myself as the leader in my marriage, but the idea that Jennifer was actually scared of me would concern me. I can't imagine a man could announce publicly that his wife was scared of him without someone dialing 911 as soon as he left the room, but she did it so casually that he really must be scared of her. Wow, just wow.

There are of course dominant women and submissive men out there, so a marriage between them can be quite functional and happy. Plenty of men pay good money to lick mistress's boots while she whips them, so clearly there's a market out there for submissive men and a place for dominant women as well. As long as no one is hurt I don't really care what people do behind closed doors. The life you lead is yours; I'm just offering advice here. I've never said that husband-led monogamous marriage is the only way to live, it's just a strategy of living and I expound on that strategy so it can be played to your best advantage.

Even so... I had a distinct feeling that if I had said "Well if you ever want to be with a man that isn't scared of you..." and given her a naughty boy smile, she would have just laughed it off. But also that her Rationalization Hamster might have started up about me every so often. Maybe once a month or so...

I didn't though. We weren't in private so her anti-slut defense would have activated and it would have backfired. Plus to be quite honest, Jennifer is hotter.

53 - If You Want A Personal Fuck Toy You Have To Be Willing To Be An Asshole

December 16, 2010

One of the primary insights of the Game viewpoint - and truthfully this is just basic behavioral analysis rather than specific to Game - is not that you stop listening to women, but that you pay attention to their actions as their actual message.

For example imagine if a mom is in a grocery store with a toddler asking for candy. The mom says "No" and the toddler starts crying. The mom says "No" again and the crying gets louder and louder until finally the mom relents and buys the candy. The verbal message here is "No candy", but the actual message from her actions is "If you cry I will give you candy." As a result the kid throws a fit for candy every time they go to the grocery store. If she just calmly listens to the tears and leaves the store, the kid has to follow or be left behind. The message then is "No candy, and crying doesn't work."

Unfortunately most men are dumber than toddlers when it comes to women. Usually when a man hears a woman say "I just want to meet a nice guy, why can't I meet a nice guy?" he actually believes that she wants to meet a Nice Guy. So he becomes a Nice Guy to try and attract and please her. When she starts dating another asshole similar to the last guy she complained about, the Nice Guy is confused and hurt. (That was a basic summary of my dating life before Jennifer.)

Thus the Game insight "stop listening to what women say and start paying attention to what they do" is a brilliant thought to most men. Very frequently women say they want a "sweet kind nice man", but then they repeatedly date someone considerably harsher in personality. The real message is "I am attracted to strong men." Or probably more correctly, "I am attracted to strong men but I want them to be nice to just me and not dump me for someone else."

Once men get that basic understanding that modeling interpersonal strength attracts women and they start putting it into practice, they are almost always absolutely stunned at how much more women pay them attention. In truth women can pooh-pooh this point as much as they like, all a man has to do is take it for a whirl for six months and they will become a convert.

For the most part the social dominance resulting from Game is fairly simple, it's not about making the woman do anything or controlling her at all, it's about making her replaceable by another woman. The correct frame is that a woman doesn't have to do anything for you at all. If she wants to be with you she can, if she wants to have sex with you she can, if she wants to play house and raise your kids she can. But if she doesn't want to do any of that, there's another woman (or women) waiting in the wings that would. The essence of Game is giving yourself options. If your Saturday is a decision between Cheryl, Susan or Julie you're going to get laid, maybe twice. Obviously this can make a wife extremely nervous and naturally Game will be viewed with great suspicion because it advantages the husband. There doesn't even have to be an actual woman waiting in the wings like an understudy quietly poisoning the leading lady. There just has to be the skill set available to replace the leading lady with minimal inconvenience.

Game isn't about making a woman do something. It's about her missing out on you if she doesn't.

One of the primary premises of this blog is that you can't actually change the other spouse. I can't actually control or make Jennifer do anything she doesn't want to. I can only control my behavior and have that be something she responds to.

Thanks to Feminism I learned a lot of supposedly female skills over the years, so now the only thing I really need from a woman is sex. I can cook, clean, raise kids, shop, deal with illness, decorate, pay bills, make friends and entertain myself yada yada yada. Or hire people to do that for me. So the criteria for Jennifer hanging with me is that I get copious sex or I walk and find someone else that will. And I would. She knows I would. I know that she knows I would. And she knows that I know that she knows I would. Hence she becomes my personal fuck toy. (In editing the post Jennifer requested a T-Shirt with "Athol's Personal Fuck Toy" on it. At least I know what to get her for Christmas now). And once a woman is your personal fuck toy, you pretty much can get away with anything outside the bedroom. And yes, that does make me an asshole. Or at the very least, her personal asshole that is nice to her and not dumping her for anyone else.

If she's sick, exhausted or whatever and can't have sex, I totally get that. I've supported her through a number of medical incidents over the years where I just loved her, cared for her, held down the fort and jerked off for several months. I just have zero tolerance for being married to someone and not having a sex life for any proper reason. Sex is why I married. Married Man = Sex Life. I am an asshole about this, but I'm an easily understandable asshole. I really did explain this clearly before I married her.

I also can't stand dumbass people that need to be saved from themselves. That's a criteria as well. Thankfully Jennifer is a bright woman and has great common sense. I have enough stuff to do in my own day to worry about micromanaging someone else's. I also want to be with someone that's basically pleasant and enjoyable to be with. Jennifer is sweet and fun. So check on that one too.

She's a living breathing wonderful woman that I am devoted to and still in love with.

On the flip side, Jennifer has her own criteria too. I think one is exactly the same as my dumbass one, so that's no problem. Well, usually anyway lol. There's another one that's basically "You have to be nice to me and the girls and help out, or I will get quite unhappy." This one is not hard really and matches my "You gotta be pleasant" criteria as well so no problem either. We really are nice to each other.

Her other criteria is that if I get sex from anywhere else, she will walk. I haven't actually tested on this one yet. Obviously I wouldn't mind some extra candy... but she's quite good with managing toddlers.

Importantly you can't do this sort of thing where you're willing to walk because of not enough sex until you can actively attract other women. If she thinks that if you walk you're just going to be crying and humping a pillow, she won't care one wit about you trying this sort of thing.

54 - The Splinter Of Mistrust And The Quest For 50

December 17, 2010

Learning about Game and what makes affairs tick can drive you a little crazy. Just reading the stories of pick up guys talking about discovering who she really put out for while she closed up shop for them can be quite eye opening. The stuff I read on the Talk About Marriage forums has an even greater degree of chaos and drama. What people can put their spouses through is appalling.

The truth is I've just found myself trusting Jennifer less. She hasn't done anything weird or odd. I just have a compulsion to GPS tag her car, tap her phone, keylogger her computer and somehow staple a spy camera to her vagina. You know, just to be sure. Trust but verify.

For the most part I've been a quite dependable Beta over my lifetime But in relation to Jennifer I've been quite Alpha for the majority of our marriage quite unwittingly. I just was so smitten and it cost so much to be with her, that when we finally married there was such a savage intensity of devotion and unstoppable pent up desire that I came across as Alpha. The rest of the world probably saw me as quite Beta, but Jennifer got an Alpha Beta mix. Plus I believe we also have a near perfect genetic match for sexual attraction to each other so that helps too.

But looking back, apart from the sexual intensity I naturally bring, there have been long dull times where I can see expanses of endless Beta living where I was nothing but nice. Nice to her, nice to the kids, nice to my friends, nice to my job. Jennifer is also very nice so we managed to coast along being nice to each other with no real incident. But despite everything going well, I really had no clue why it was working well, and my practical Game understanding was worthless for a long, long time.

So I do at times wonder what would have happened if someone else had really singled Jennifer out years ago and just started working on her. Some other guy with more money, more muscle, a bit of a swagger and a touch of asshole. I may have been fairly defenseless to that. Knowing Jennifer I don't think she would have taken the bait, but then I've heard a couple hundred other men in the last year say exactly the same thing about their wives. (And wives saying that about their husbands too.) No no, not my angel. It's just not possible. Then the keylogger turns up the secret email account devoted to the sordid.

The stories all play out the same it seems. It starts as some incidental meeting, there's a small harmless connection made, then there's more of a connection, then the cell phone gets locked and lots of calls and texts, then there are some minor lies of omission, then larger lies, then a full scale cover up and huge emotions running hot and cold. The good wife they loved and knew gets replaced with a total stranger like some sort of alien science fiction bug had burrowed into her brain and taken control over her.

*****

From "The Quest For 50" (Blog)

Him?

She stared at me, sympathy in her eyes. "Are you okay?"

"Yes..."

"It's nothing serious, I just want someone to go with."

"Did you have sex with him?"

"Why is that your business?"

"DID YOU HAVE SEX WITH HIM?"

"YES! WHY DOES IT MATTER!"

"You said he's an asshole!"

(smiles) "He is an asshole…"

I break down in tears. I don't understand.

*****

And that's the standard conversation where a Nice Guy learns the truth about what works sexually for women.

So sometimes I do wonder "what if." What if that had all played out and Jennifer was just one day gone from me. What would I have done in the aftermath? I know I would have been utterly shattered by it for a long, long time. Now I believe if it all falls apart, I'd be deeply hurt and angered by it, then go the same route as Dagonet at Quest For 50. Of the majority of Game bloggers out there he still seems to have a sweetness about him. He seems to be set on racking up "wins" rather than "kills" if that makes any sense. My hunch is that he will meet someone special before he gets to 50 notches. That's his call though. Game is values neutral and your goal with it is up to you.

As it is, I've never had to have that conversation. For that I am profoundly grateful. Having learned what I now know I feel like I've dodged a major bullet. It's like coming out of the grocery store and finding you left your car keys in the ignition and the doors unlocked for the last ninety minutes. Nothing happened so it's cool, but damn what the hell were you thinking. The worst part of blogging on this topic and getting email from readers is occasionally I have to explain to a husband that she is already cheating on him. Sometimes they have unwittingly actively assisted with the wife's affair. I'm so sorry dude you left the keys in the car and the doors unlocked, that's why someone stole your ride.

*****

So anyway, Jennifer hates the cold, really hates it. We had gone out to dinner a few weeks ago and were headed for EB Games in the local strip mall. All the stores have doors on both the road side and the parking lot side of the store except EB Games which has the parking lot door blocked off. Coming from the parking lot in the freezing air I went to cut through the wine store...

Jennifer: "Are you going to buy something in there?"

Me: "No we're cutting through to the other side."

Jennifer made this pained face like I had just soiled myself.

Me: "Ok ok, we can go around. You're the one that hates the cold."

And we walked around the whole string of shops. Four shops up, around Starbucks at the end and past the same four shops back. It's so freaking, freaking cold. I tease her a little as we walk this stupid route. Well maybe more mocking than teasing. She just couldn't offend the wine store retail clerk by walking through the store and not buying something lol. I was possibly a little mean to her about it. *Possibly*.

So anyway, we collect World of Warcraft: Cataclysm and ahead back out. This time we just start walking around the stores, doing that big loop in the chill air and I find myself having one of those moments of perfect understanding. Even when she doesn't want to do the right thing, when no one would really care if she didn't and someone is egging her on to do the wrong thing, she always does the right thing anyway.

It was like finally getting a splinter out. I felt a wave of relief and a little silly for ever not fully trusting her.

Jennifer: "Whhhhhaaaaaat?"

Me: "Oh nothing."

We walked to the car, eldest daughter in tow. Once in the car I tossed Jennifer my hat because it was warm from my head.

Me: "Warm up your hands in my hat."

That made her ridiculously happy and she smiled and giggled at me like we were standing in line for the roller coaster at Knoebels in 1991. I'm still hooked on that giggle.

So anyway, our Quest For 50 continues. Jennifer and I are in year 17.

55 - Fried Tofu Explain Yourself

December 19, 2010

So we had our Nursing Christmas party / December staff meeting at a restaurant called "It's Only Natural." It sounded good to me because I'm just fine with natural foods. If things get too processed they just aren't all that nice and half the chain restaurants load up everything with MSG anyway which... well, let's just say my body has a well established violent protocol for MSG exposure. So I'm excited about the party...

... and I get there and it's freaking vegetarian bordering on vegan.

Do. Not. Want.

Seriously how many men like to celebrate a hard year's work with something made from soy??? I know it's just one meal, but this was meant to be a "thank you", not a "you won't mind will you" event. I get that what doesn't kill me makes me stronger, but soy increases estrogen production in men so stronger might be a debatable point. I don't want to push away from the dinner table thinking, "Boy my nipples are sensitive today."

Fried Tofu explain yourself - what is the point of your existence except to give the Female Rationalization Hamster something to gnaw on? Why are the waitresses so pudgy? If this is an ultra healthy restaurant, why do the wait staff look fat? Why does everyone have so many tattoos here that a pirate would feel self-conscious? Damn it why can't I have a soda? If I'm going to get diabetes I want to do it drinking soda and not peach and carrot juice. I didn't even know carrots had juice.

Pretty much every year around Christmas I get the default gift from whoever the Nursing Director is, and simply come home and hand it to Jennifer. Fancy soap, fancy lotion, special little trinket, yada yada yada, it's all girly stuff every year. Whatever, Jennifer and I just laugh about it and she gets a free gift for putting up with me. If the gift is really daft we just re-gift it to Nana.

But I skipped breakfast to save room for a yummy lunch. So I had to eat something and got whole wheat pizza with sautéed onions, Portobello mushrooms and a sprinkle of parmesan cheese. In the defense of the chef it obviously came out exactly as they intended. They didn't cook it badly, it was just a seriously misguided creation. It would have been infinitely better for cheese and sausage and a thinner crunchy crust. The onions could go as well, but if I scraped all those off all I'd have left is a whole wheat Frisbee.

So anyway it's food, so whatever, I can survive a lunch. Mostly though, I don't like being made to feel like a "male nurse" by people I think of as my friends. Especially after all the work I've done to make things better and easier for them all. Grrrr.

I texted Jennifer when I was walking in that it was vegetarian. She texted back "LOL" and that she was eating hamburgers in McDonald's. So Jennifer +1, women I work with -2. Damn I hope my book sells a ton of copies....

And OMG when does the farting stop?

56 - Men Are Incapable Of Lying After Orgasm

December 20, 2010

Reader Email: I'm in a fairly new relationship and my guy was joking (I think) that in the couple of minutes immediately after orgasm, a guy is incapable of lying. So he says I should use that opportunity to ask him anything.

First, could this actually be true? Like I said, I'm pretty sure he's just kidding around but it got me wondering...

Second, if you could ask your SO one question and they HAD to answer honestly, what would it be? Doesn't have to be anything too deep, something silly is good too.

Athol: Why the hell would it be true?

Oh hang on....

.... a masked figure dressed in black enters the small prison cell. He stands menacingly over the rebel alliance soldier with labored artificial breathing. Darth Vader waves off the Interrogation Droid and produces a small bottle of lotion, its soft aroma of strawberries slowly scenting the cell.

"I'm asking you for the last time, where is the rebel base?"

"I'll never tell you! NEVER!"

"Very well you leave me no choice...."

"OMG NO! Not that!!!!"

fap fap fap fap fap fap fap fap fap fap SQUIRT!

"Now where is the rebel base?"

"It's on Dantooine in the Raioballo sector of the Outer Rim. But you'll need these pass codes to get past the outer defense screens..."

Vader contacts Grand Moff Tarkin via comlink, "I have extracted information from one of the prisoners that the rebel base is on Dantooine."

Tarkin pauses then responds, "Dantooine is too remote to make an effective demonstration. See if you can extract more information from the prisoner."

"Well we already extracted quite a lot of information from the prisoner," said Vader absentmindedly wiping some of the information off his chest plate, "he may need to rest for a little bit."

Tarkin frowns, "use any means necessary."

Vader simply nods and produces a moderately sized silicon attachment and screws it into the base of his lightsaber while eyeing the rebel scum with malevolence. Once done he ignites the saber and the silicon attachment glows red and vibrates furiously with a hum that transfixes the rebel and quickens his breath in anticipation of talking a great deal more...

As to the second question. I would ask... "Tell me what you've lied to me about before now...."

57 - Don't Be A White Knight, Be A Horny Knight

December 22, 2010

Periodically women get into a spot of bother and can very much appreciate a spot of rescue.

My thought is that it's a fairly natural reaction to just swoop in and save them. After all that's what fairy tales are all about, the dashing white knight rescuing the damsel in distress and living happily ever after.

But like the old female advice to "don't give the milk away for free or no one will buy the cow..."

... "don't supply rescue for free or no one will give it up for the knight."

It's perfectly fine to rescue women, just frame it from the get go as "I'm not a white knight, I'm a horny knight. Do you wish to be rescued?" If the answer is "no", then thumbs up to feminism and you can skip the effort of saving her. By jumping directly to the end point of not having sex with her, you incur minimal wastage of your day.

Of course in a marriage, both husband and wife are going to get into a spot of bother once in a while and desire a spot of rescue. Why shouldn't you both get to play a game of Horny Knight to the Rescue? "Sure honey, I'll come unlock your car for you. But you've got to hand over your underwear..."

And of course people that require endless rescuing for no good reason are basically awful as spouses. If you're constantly saving a girlfriend from her own folly, marrying her is like becoming her unpaid support staff.

58 - Don't Cater Endlessly To A SAHM

January 1, 2011

The back story to this one is that the SAHM is bored in her $400,000 home and has an affair started via Facebook that the husband has just discovered. The unfolding story is that he's been doing the standard Betaized Nice Guy routine to... well to a fault...

"I guess you can say that, yep things aren't done around the house but she says I need to do more! Well I've spoiled her it's my fault. I would think women would like to be spoiled and love you for it!!"

Yes you would think that women would love you for spoiling them, but it turns out they see you as a weakling for doing so. If you keep running up to them and giving them nice things, they see that as you trying to seek to keep the relationship stable because you are not as attractive as they are.

I.e. if you're a 7 and she's an 8, you endlessly being nice to her is seen as you trying to be a 7 and +1 point for being endlessly nice = her 8.

You could be a 9 to an impartial observer, but you running up to her and being endlessly nice means she would still perceive you as a lesser value, because of the endless catering to her. She just sees "endless catering = +1", so "hubby +1 = my worth", therefore "hubby worth < my worth", therefore "I deserve this affair because I am better than hubby and I am sooooo bored."

So if you endlessly cater to her, she will see you as a man that she could do better than. It's not until the shit hits the fan and all the good you do starts getting threatened to be taken away, will she realize the more realistic value between you both. If it turns out that you're in fact a better man than she is a woman, she will crawl back to you and beg forgiveness. Though you have to decide if you want her back. Her cheating on you does tend to somewhat reduce her Sex Rank value in and of itself.

Obviously you can't keep her on as a lazy SAHM and cheating wife, so she will have to make some improvements or suffer the consequences.

In any case, isn't the job description of a SAHM that she caters to you?

59 - Sexy Move: Maybe She'd Love A Facial

January 3, 2011

I'm not sure how it started, but the common scene ender in porn is for the man to ejaculate onto the woman's face. Sometimes you can see the woman just scrunching her face up and trying to find her happy place when it happens. One would think that anything that makes porn people grossed out is generally really nasty. I hate getting to the end of a good scene and then the porn-babe looks like she's trying not to cry and barf. I really don't react well to women doing something sexual they don't want to do, total boner killer. So yeah I'm a softy I admit it. Plus a couple times in my career as a nurse I've had "fluids" squirted in my direction without my prior consent. (Do. Not. Want.) So as a result I always disliked the idea of cumming on Jennifer's face as being offensive and humiliating.

Anyway... one day several months back we were doing the routine handjob and cumming on her breasts plan which Jennifer is fabulous at. But we had skipped getting me off the day before, so there was a little extra payload to be delivered. Plus I was also a little more worked up than usual and when I orgasmed I cannoned an enormous stream of semen in a single massive pulse. In a combination of glee and horror I watched a glorious volley of warm white fly well beyond any hope of touching her breasts; up her chin, across her mouth, from the tip to the bridge of her nose, between her eyes, up her forehead and then into a low earth orbit.

Jennifer just lay lay there doing an imitation of a blind goldfish that had accidentally jumped out of the fish bowl. Eyes clenched shut, open mouthed and gasping. Oh shit... now I've really done it.

Then she giggled...

I had a small mental implosion over that giggle for about three months. Sometimes even to me women make no sense whatsoever. But I fell back on the old standby of "don't worry about what women say, pay attention to what they do." She giggled, so that means she liked it. But that couldn't possibly be true could it. Damn this is weird. This was not covered by anything I ever read in my whole life.

I was still semi-embarrassed by it, but I found myself secretly hoping that I would repeat the same event. Then not so secretly hoping. I started edging upwards a little more each time with the-cum-on-her-breasts routine and trying to angle myself just right... and she didn't seem to fight it off at all. Bizarre.

Eventually I asked for a completely properly planned facial and she basically laughed at me for taking so long to ask for it. It's still something I feel funny about asking for though as I guess old habits die hard and I don't want to overuse it as something to do. Anyway fast forward a few months and we've planned for facials a few times. Unfortunately it's semi-hopeless as I cum absolute buckets and our aim is terrible. The headboard... her shoulder... the carpet... her pillow...

So while I can say with a high level of confidence that it is not for everyone, maybe it would liven up a dull evening as a trial just for fun. And like I say often – only about 30% of what you try in bed together will work. If it doesn't work, then wipe it off with a warm washcloth, admit you hated it and try something else.

Oh and do NOT get it in your eyes as it stings like hell. I'm okay now though.

60 - I Broke The Second Date Rule

January 5, 2011

Badger Nation (Edit: One of my blog friends) asked me a few days back in a comment about me breaking "The Second Date Rule" with Jennifer when I stopped being an Evangelical Christian and became an Atheist. The Second Date Rule being "If I just saw behavior like that on the second date, would I have ever had a third date with this person?"

The answer to that question is yes indeed I did very much break the second date rule. I more than broke it, I shattered it. I had been sent off to a private Christian school at age 7 and converted to an Evangelical faith at age 16. I started work for The Bible Society in New Zealand at age 20 and quit a year later to work on a summer camp in Maryland. Viki, one of my new American friends on the camp liked my perspective on discipleship as a teaching strategy. Being unstoppable in personality, Viki convinced her college Chaplain to let me come and teach a weekend discipleship retreat in conjunction with the college chapel.

So at age 21 and my religious faith peaking, I taught two days worth of sessions to a smallish group of people at the college. Jennifer sat front and center with her eyes shining up at me for the entire thing. After the teaching weekend was done, I had another six or so days left in America before my flight back to New Zealand so I stayed on the campus sleeping on the dorm room floor with two of the guys I had taught. In a very Christ-like way I broke up Jennifer and her boyfriend...

After that it was back to New Zealand for me and I grieved what could have been if we were in the same country. I was still moping about when a few months later Jennifer sent me a care package and it was on between us and has been ever since. Three years later Viki was Jennifer's maid of honor and the college Chaplain married us. We started our new life together and all was well. But during those three years apart, I had thought a great deal more about faith and had started to not merely have questions, but really probing struggles with things. I had made an active choice not to do something like a Bible College and completed my Sociology degree instead. My concern was that if I ever lost my faith, a Bible College diploma would be useless towards employment.

Sometime in the first year of our marriage I became totally disenchanted with Christianity, I don't mean to sidetrack this post with the "why", please just accept that it did. My church attendance dropped off and eventually it stopped.

The worst thing was telling Jennifer. I really wasn't sure what would happen to us. Obviously she knew something was up with me because I wasn't attending church and I purposefully picked up Sunday shifts to avoid the issue. Plus at that point if we divorced I wasn't yet at the two year mark for applying for citizenship and I'd lose my Visa and likely be deported. So telling her the truth was a huge risk, but an honest one.

When I told her, she completely broke down and just sobbed. Not just crying, but anguished sobbing into my chest and I cried too for her pain. I believe I did the right thing, I had never lied about my questioning belief and she knew about it, but she had hope that I would resolve them in favor of having faith. I'd gone from someone that shone with faith and had taught her, to someone that simply didn't believe. I very much hurt her in that moment.

What happened after that was going to be 100% up to Jennifer. I had done nothing purposely wrong, but I accepted the blame as the party in the wrong. I answered all her questions, I supported her going to church, I never spoke badly of her faith, and I didn't try and convert her to Atheism despite a huge desire to do so. The only thing I didn't do was attend church with her. Otherwise I made no changes in my behavior; I stayed faithful to her and was a good husband.

Thankfully I have a very forgiving wife. It was awkward for a number of months, but ultimately I didn't sprout horns and turn nasty on her. Truthfully I am a kinder, happier, calmer, relaxed and more engaged person for being an Atheist; I became a better man for my change. If she had relentlessly hounded me and hated me for being Atheist, ultimately I would have left her in sorrow, but she stayed to me the same sweet girl I knew.

Somehow we just muddled through. We got a house together, we had a kid. She was promoted several times, I did nursing school. We had another kid and fixed up the house. When we baptized the kids I was absolutely against it, but never said a word and went to church to keep the peace. When her family say grace at family meals I scrunch up inside and hate it, but I never say a word and keep the peace; even in my own house.

Over time things have changed on Jennifer's end as well. Her religious position has softened greatly and her church attendance is different now too, and that's all I have a right to say about her belief. I devoted myself to us and raising our kids. I've worked for a non-profit with the developmentally disabled as a nurse for the better part of 15 years. I'm not a believer in God or the Bible, but for a lack of a better word, my life has been "Christian." Writing this blog I've had several people mistakenly believe that I am a believer in God simply because I'm helpful, family orientated and not cheating on my wife. I just take it as a compliment and enjoy their surprise when I do the reveal.

But by the same token, while I stopped believing in God in 1995, I didn't publicly "come out" as an Atheist out of respect for Jennifer until 2010. It hurt sometimes along the way, but I always wanted to make sure I made it to the third date.

The thing I miss the most about being in church is the preaching. I love public speaking and I love teaching. I love communicating and helping. I'm quite aware that what I'm doing now with the blog is nearly exactly what I was doing twenty years ago, but with different content. I do have goals for this thing I'm doing beyond books…

… but mostly just I want to look down into the front row and see her eyes shining up at me.

61 - SAHM's Need To Be SAHM's "Plus Something."

January 6, 2011

Seeing I was a Stay At Home Dad, I get asked about the SAHM thing once in a while. Here's my story first, then the opinion section...

When Jennifer and I married, we decided that I would come to America rather than her go to New Zealand. One reason was that we decided that I would cope better at being away from my family, than her being away from hers. Nowadays we could probably just as easily go either way, but back in the day Jennifer was more timid with travel than I was.

The other reason was that despite us being able to have a fairly similar lifestyle in each country, there are significant exchange rate differences between New Zealand and America. So if we ever wanted to sell up and switch countries down the line, moving from New Zealand to America would have us arrive broke, and America to New Zealand would have us arrive in comfort.

So penniless with nothing but a suitcase, a small backpack, winning charm and a hard on, I arrived in America and we married. However what we didn't really realize was that switching countries was going to affect my career. Well the career I didn't even have yet anyway. My Sociology Degree was near useless plus I didn't know anyone here for letters of reference. In the end when I finally got a job, it was with Jennifer's company. My credential was basically Jennifer. She was a pleasant and good worker, so as her husband, they just assumed I was much the same.

For the first few years of our marriage Jennifer out earned me and out ranked me in our company. I was turned down repeatedly for promotions, so I decided to step around the roadblock. So me and 400 of my best friends applied to the state nursing program for 1 of 40 places. I got into nursing school and apparently I also got into Jennifer as well... she got pregnant. So I did nursing school while still working full time on a nights and weekends split shift pattern. We had eldest daughter halfway through nursing school and plopped her into daycare. That way Jennifer could go back to work as soon as maternity leave was done and I could finish school. Day care was expensive and we were bailed out of losing the house by her parents.

As soon as school was done there was only one logical thing to do... we instantly pulled eldest from daycare and I stayed home during the week to look after her. Jennifer worked during the week and then we switched off for the weekend and I did nights and weekends 24-32 hours a week. Based on this awesome plan, Jennifer got pregnant again. Then she miscarried almost immediately, but I figured out a way to stop her crying about the miscarriage. I am the Baby Sniper; one shot, one hospital bill.

The second pregnancy was very difficult. Jennifer was in and out of the ER every week for about four months. She only avoided bed rest in the hospital because her OB remembered me from the first birth and I was both a nurse and the SAHD. Otherwise, she would have been hospitalized for four months. Daughter number two was clearly bored and Jennifer went from 4cm dilated to complete birth in 15 minutes. She missed her window for pain meds and did the whole thing natural. I know this because she tore my left arm off because I said "push" inappropriately.

So I still had the weekend/night job, Jennifer still had the day job. We had two kids. So I stayed home and watched them during the day and she did the weekend. It was all quite logical. I don't know how we could have done it differently. Youngest did give me absolute hell for not having breast milk and yes Jennifer pumped it out and we bottled it and youngest was clear that there was just NO WAY THAT WOULD WORK EVER. She'd scream all day every day until Jennifer came home. She finally broke and took a bottle from me on day 6 of the scream-a-thon and then everything was good at home for a while. Then youngest got sick.

I'm not posting what her issue was, but she did have something that made her very cranky and very behavior driven. It took about six months to get to the bottom of it with multiple meds and doctors. Once we figured it out the cure was fairly quickly in place, but it then took about eighteen months of active management to get to the point where it had resolved completely. I was pretty exhausted by this point and we had eldest in some daycare programs for play purposes part time. Once she was in kindergarten, youngest was lonely and bored and we transitioned her into daycare full time as well.

When I finally was free of both kids during the day, I eventually got switched into a day position at work. Finally after about six years of pregnancies and toddlers, we all graduated together into being a family with everyone being on a regular schedule.

The job that I worked was group home based and with developmentally disabled adults. My job involved making a home and caring for people with enormous needs of personal care. My job involved an eight hour shift of medicating, cooking, cleaning, bathing, changing, teaching, medical appointments, state inspections, staff meetings, outings, and meeting federal guidelines for "Active Treatment."

In comparison to all that, having a pair of toddlers play with each other and going to the park once Oprah was done... well the SAHD routine was easy. Changing diapers on a two year old is easy compared to an adult that doesn't want to be bothered with it right now. A one year old can be given a snack and eat it safely; my work clients could suck breakfast into their lungs and get pneumonia, so they were total feeds, or on feeding tubes. A kid can get dressed themselves; my clients needed help dressing and getting into wheelchairs.

Being the SAHD was never something I expected to do in life. It was a unique experience and something that I am forever grateful for. I adore my children and I think those early years together made a huge difference in the way we have bonded. Also my kids are well behaved, so I am proud of that too. To be sure my job very much helped my parenting skills and outlook. I always saw my kids as being easy to care for, so maybe that's why they were.

Our house was a little group home where we just planned it out so the girls could do things for themselves. For example, their beds were mattresses on the floor so they could get in and out easily, and no one worried about them falling out of the bed. We had organized clothing racks. Out house was tiny, so we moved our bedroom into the girls' room and the girls and all their toys into our bigger bedroom. They could take only one or two toys out of their bedroom to play, after that it needed to go back into the bedroom. Ah my nice clean living room... so free of clutter and kids' crap.

To be sure Jennifer did her part too. When I worked the weekend and nights, I was exhausted beyond all reason. She basically did it all on the weekend and tip toed the kids around my sleeping body and snuck them quietly out of the house to the mall, to the park, just out. We were a tag team and a good one. Though one of the biggest fights of our marriage happened after Jennifer and the girls ruined my nice clean house one weekend, and I had to clean it all back up during the week.

Sex was always a requirement though. The mornings I came home from nights and needed to sleep, I'd start myself off and get myself 95% of the way to orgasm. Jennifer would hand out cheerios in cups to the kids as a distraction and sneak into the bedroom. The usual finish was a sixty second blowjob. It doesn't sound exciting but you try masturbating to the brink of orgasm for fifteen minutes and have a randomly timed finish by oral; it's pretty intense. In any case, sex stayed on the menu and never came off it. Something is better than nothing and we stayed in sexual contact with each other through a long hard grind.

So anyway, there we go, I've done the SAHD thing for about four years solid. Plus I worked, plus I had a sick kid, so there... I'm all done on building credibility.

My trouble with SAHM's is not that they are SAHM's, but that some of them take the position as a form of early retirement. Please believe me when I say that the job of raising your own kids in your own house is a pretty soft job. If you're truly whining that it is "real work", then you're terrible at it. You aren't living in the 1800s and fetching water, knitting and making shoes; that is "real work." For most people at home with their kids on their non-working days, it's called "not being at work." Most men make perfectly adequate on-duty parents just as soon as their wives get out of the way and stop telling them how they are doing it wrong.

I think being a SAHM or SAHD is a perfectly acceptable plan to bridge small children into the school age years. It can make economic good sense to do so, us being not bankrupt was a great idea that I fully supported. But clearly there's just not enough to do all day at home without going crazy. I think you've got to be a SAHM plus something to be pulling your weight. Whether that something is; a part time job, a stay at home business that actually makes money, more education for you in the evening, or actively supporting and pushing the career of the working spouse further than they could have gone solo, it all works - just do plus-something. By "actively supporting" I mean you're throwing dinner parties, you're doing the 500 Christmas card list "from him", you're the one that sends out happy birthday notes "from him" for his contacts, when he has a sick employee you're the one that sends over the tray of goodies "from him." That sort of thing. Actively supporting doesn't mean that you just watch TV while he studies for a master's degree.

The trap for husbands with a SAHM is pretty real. If she works out and does the SAHM role well, it can work out very well for both of them. But there is a real moral hazard in that it can be a soft job and de facto early retirement. There is no way to "fire" a SAHM because it isn't a "real job." The threshold of failure as a SAHM is having the state take your children from you for neglect. In comparison most minimum wage jobs fire you for simply being late half a dozen times. A husband watching his bride devolve into a lazy worthless screechtard has made the very worst mistake of his life. To leave her he will, via alimony and child support, continue to pay her for the job she wasn't doing in the first place.

My advice to men with new SAHM's is to be cautious and watch what she does with the first kid. If she's a SAMH plus something, then you're probably ok. She's a keeper. Really, many women are just great wives and mothers. There are good ones out there. There are plenty of women that will totally get this post and will feel vindicated for reading it and who hate the lazy SAHM's that make them look awful by association.

But if she's a SAHM plus whining....

...you need to address that sooner rather than later.

62 - Christmas Tree Removal 101

January 9, 2011

Christmas Tree Removal 101.

(1) Get bins from the basement and drop them by the tree.

(2) Tell kids to put the tree and Christmas junk in the bins.

(3) Have a shower while the minions work.

(4) Take bins of crap back down to the basement.

(5) Fish through bins for the automatic Elvis singing thing that the kids love, but drives me crazy, and discard it.

(6) Next year claim that the kids packed the tree so I don't want to hear about the missing Elvis.

63 - Play Blue's Clues or Maybe You Lose

January 10, 2011

I hang out on The About Marriage forum a lot and have noticed a fairly frequent pattern of the story of a man losing his wife or having her caught up in an affair. To be fair, there's about an equal number of stories of wives losing their husbands, but I tend to focus on the guys to be honest.

So anyway it all goes like this:

Phase One: "Hey I've noticed that my wife has been doing *list of blindingly obvious things pointing to an affair* is this something to worry about?"

Then the board tells them to keylogger her computer, GPS tag her car, put a motion activated camera somewhere, yada yada yada...

Phase Two: "OMG you guys were right!!!! She was doing it with *my best friend / her boss / old boyfriend / loser with muscles* what do I do?"

Then the board trots out the standard gather evidence, expose, Plan A break it off (carrot and stick), or Plan B social nuking, and if that fails divorce.

Phase Three: Actually phase three takes a while and goes around and around for about one to six months as the affair fallout plays itself out. There's ups, there's downs, there's drama galore and sometimes it all comes together and sometimes it just doesn't. Usually the board does pretty well though and eventually it moves into whatever way it resolves finally as Phase Four.

Phase Four: "Actually about three years ago my wife wrote me letters a couple times saying how miserable and unhappy she was in the marriage."

Oy....

Back in the day I used to watch Blue's Clues with the kids. It seems like a tearful letter from a wife to a husband needs to come with a big blue paw print on it. What's that, Blue? Have you found a clue?

I'm not saying that the husband ignoring blindingly obvious clues justifies the wife having an affair or leaving him. I'm just saying most women don't just "suddenly" turn feral on the man they walked down the aisle with. Maybe picking up on a red flag early on could save a lot of grief... and money.

64 - The Propinquity Effect: A Third Wheel In Your Own Home Is You Being Stupid

January 22, 2011

You always need to be very cautious about having friends living with you as a married couple for an extended length of time. When your buddy visits and stays as a guest, there's usually a lot of close interaction between you and your friend as you make the best use of your time together. But what you call "hanging out and having a beer" also doubles up with what evolutionary psychologists call "mate guarding behavior." Or in plain English, you're having fun with your friend, but you're also cockblocking your friend getting to your wife.

But if you let your buddy actually start living with you, there's no way to maintain the cockblock. You can't just hang out and have a beer every single day when there's real life and working late heading up your personal chore list. So at some point your buddy and your wife are going to be left together minus you. Now it's unlikely that as your car pulls out of the driveway leaving them alone for the very first time, that they will lock eyes across the cornflakes and head back to your bedroom for five hours. But if you give it a couple of months just about anything can happen.

Now I know someone is going to say, "Awww not my friend, I can trust him."

Well no. No you can't. You're an idiot. You can't trust him because he is your friend.

From Wikipedia...

"In social psychology, propinquity (from Latin propinquitas, nearness) is one of the main factors leading to interpersonal attraction. It refers to the physical or psychological proximity between people. Propinquity can mean physical proximity, a kinship between people, or a similarity in nature between things. Two people living on the same floor of a building, for example, have a higher propinquity than those living on different floors, just as two people with similar political beliefs possess a higher propinquity than those whose beliefs strongly differ."

Having a friend hanging out with your wife in your house is just a huge propinquity effect both because he is physically close to her and also psychologically close to her; he's already accepted and positively regarded. Even if he gets under her skin a bit it's a bad thing, that just means he emotionally engages her and he looms in her psyche. She may have minimal interest in him romantically at the start, but a few months into him living with you, it would be extremely unusual if she didn't develop deeper feelings for him. Once that happens you've got two people with sexual motive, a bedroom and the perfect alibi for being alone in your house together.

Queue up... "What the hell?! You said you didn't even like him and didn't want him here!"

Oh and I'm just assuming that your buddy wants to bang your wife. Though I've got $100 that says "maybe I get some" was one of the top two reasons he wanted to live with you in the first place. Not that there's anything wrong with that, it's a perfectly reasonable impulse for him to have if your wife is even halfway attractive. I'm just staying that I wouldn't balance a little red gas can on top of the electrical panel is all.

And of course all this plays out just the same from your wife's end should she ever ask you to have one of her friends stay over for an extended period of time. Automatically as soon as the question is asked you're going to immediately think "maybe I'll get some" and probably agree if she's even halfway attractive. Enough time living with your wife's friend and even Steve Urkel could break her down. Well maybe not Steve Urkel, but you should be able to... especially if you screw your wife extra hard and make her orgasm loudly so her friend can hear it each night...

...anyway, before I derail this post into a fantasy experience about juggling two women in my own home, let's just say no one ever stays over for too long at our place. I'd like to be helpful if she had friend that needed to stay for a while, but in the end I just know I can't be trusted with that much temptation.

65 - Sexy Move: Ask For Her Special Dish

January 23, 2011

Most wives have something they are really good at doing and you like whatever that thing is she does. So ask for it once in a while.

Usually that special thing is making some sort of food. Let's face it, most of us are not chefs and we turn out quite edible food but on average it's all quite mundane. But usually she will have a small handful of things that she's really, really good at making, but she only makes them for special occasions.

So just ask for it anyway. And then you eat it. Slowly. Ideally sitting with her.

Once done eating you say, "I don't really understand why, but when you make this I just get this wonderful feeling inside that we're a family."

You should get some sort of positive reaction from that one as it tugs on her heartstrings. So enjoy the moment of warm fuzzies and cuddle and kiss. Once that starts to settle down a little say in your best I'm a naughty boy voice, "It also makes me horny."

Jennifer makes me sausage rolls once in a while. They are basically sausage wrapped in pastry in a long roll, cut into 2-3 inch long pieces and baked. Sausage rolls are a traditional party staple in New Zealand and it's one of the very few things that I get homesick for. Jennifer was originally stressed out by making them seeing that bad sausage rolls are a divorceable offense in New Zealand. Her first few batches were a difficult time for us.

66 - Sexting The Wife

January 26, 2011

Jennifer has to work late a couple times a week doing open houses, and detests open houses where nobody comes. She gets bored and we tend to text a little during her events where no one shows up, just to stay in contact with each other. She does a lot of events like this in her job and if they are dead it's just a vacuum, so I fill it and make her laugh. If the event is good I cheerleader her too.

When she's working late I usually make sure the house is clean, dinner done, kids happy yada yada yada in her absence. This particular night the dinner option was leftover sausage bread, but I wrangled eldest daughter into cooking pasta with me and we had that instead.

My text game with Jennifer is just to stay in playful contact and let her know that everything is going well at home. She gets mommy guilt sometimes so I think it reassures her that the kids are happy. There's a lot of Beta in the text and what I'm doing at home, but there's a firm Alpha note as well.

Me: How is it?

She: Aargh. Hate open houses when nobody comes. Leaving at 715.

Me: :-(

She: Yep. Suckage. Need sausage bread.

He: Or eldest's pasta.

She: Oh really? :-)

Me: Ya we did fetathingy and chicken

She: LOL

Me: The password to open the garage door is I WANT YOUR COCK. Just text and it's done.

She: :-)

Half an hour later...

She: I WANT YOUR COCK.

Then I opened the garage door so she didn't have to get out of the car in the snow and haul the door up. We kissed in the garage, then as she walked up the stairs into the house ahead of me I gave her a playful swat on the ass.

67 - Life Sucks, The Marriage Still Good

February 13, 2011

I've said a number of times that, "Sometimes we win and sometimes we lose, but we win and we lose as a team."

Jennifer and I are a real couple and our sex life is one of our strongest points. Our other strong point is that we communicate with each other really well, with sort of mental telepathy at times.

Because mental telepathy is probably completely infallible, we assume we never miscommunicate... which means when we do miscommunicate with each other, we can go for months before realizing that a miscommunication has happened.

Last weekend some of that miscommunication caught up with us and we had a very difficult conversation with each other. We resolved the issue as best we could and just had a stressful week. This Friday we discovered that last weekend's issue was just the fairly large part of a smallish iceberg. We've had a horrible weekend.

Some of it was her fault, some of it was my fault, so we bypassed blaming each other and just worked on solutions. We're moving on from this together and everything will be okay soon enough. Ultimately it was a good thing to have discovered what was going on. I'd write about the issues in specific, but I don't want people to try and dig into the issues and try and psychoanalyze them or try and assign fault with a running commentary either here or on other blogs. We have very much used the Forgiving and Non-Envious tactics this weekend, so case closed.

So like I said, Jennifer and I are a real couple and just like everyone else we have crappy days in our life too. We still held each other, still said we loved each other, and yes we still had sex on Friday night (she squirted), Saturday night (she cried), Sunday morning (she tolerated it) and Sunday night looks good too (she's gonna go for the handjob option when I offer it).

I've always felt that Jennifer and I are a special couple and that we have a purpose greater than us for being together. Just don't think that we are a perfect couple... or even perfect for each other. But we are married, so we will just have to make do with our choice in each other. The difference between thinking you have a crappy life and a crappy marriage is sometimes subtle, but it's there.

68 - A Short Message From the Rationalization Hamster

February 19, 2011

Here's the scenario...

After being married for a while, things slow down in the bedroom a little. Okay, say they slow down a lot. There's no real conflict happening, just a sexual slow down.

Then one day there's a little more sexual energy happening because the wife is now working with someone she finds quite attractive. She's coming home from work already warmed up and the sex at home improves. So it's a good thing. (Right?)

Having noticed the sexual charge from the attraction to a particular guy, it's very easy and tempting to make a bit of a fantasy out of the wife having sex with him. So you try it and wow is the sex amazing that night, she's wet, wild and willing like she hasn't been for years.

So it becomes a regular fantasy talked about in bed.

Then one day she just comes home all excited, states she wants sex, climbs on top of you and goes crazy just bouncing on your cock. On one hand it's over the top hot and on the other hand you know something isn't right about it. So you ask what's going on...

...but deep down you already know what happened. The fantasy got switched into a reality and she had sex with him.

So now what? You never gave her permission to do that. But you know you've encouraged it. The sex was amazing, but you want to throw up. Who's right? Who's wrong? And most importantly, will she stop having sex with him?

This one is going to be harsh...

/press conference on

The Rationalization Hamster team met this afternoon and after a long session of deliberation, it was decided that anything said in bed while having sex, "as a hot fantasy", about your wife having sex with other men, is either a statement of permission seeking or a statement of permission giving in reality. Any unfortunate miscommunication of these statements should be decided in favor of the wife that has surprise sex with someone else, as clear permission was reasonably presumed granted and she only did this initially to please her husband, by fulfilling his own request. Furthermore it is unreasonable to request a woman to stop a sexual relationship that has already started, based solely on the insecurity of the less sexually attractive male. Once her feelings have been engaged, she does not have direct control over them, so regardless of prior intent before the surprise sex to not have an ongoing relationship, her feelings would continue whether that relationship was allowed to continue or not. As such, the best course of action would be to allow the relationship to follow a natural arc of progression without interference, in hopes that her feelings self-resolve over time. While the team accepts that we have come to this point inadvertently and there is some concern for what may happen in the future, please accept the full assurance of the Rationalization Hamster team, that she has no serious intentions of abandoning the marriage.

/press conference off

In short, encouraging her to have sex with someone else to save your sex life is a terrible idea. You're meant to guard the chicken coop, not talk the chickens into visiting the fox.

69 - Cynical Advice on Responsible Non-Monogamy

February 20, 2011

I've been asked about "responsible non-monogamy" a couple times over the last few months. I don't advise stepping into this realm, but should you decide to venture there, let me give you this somewhat cynical advice...

Whether it be cuckolding, swinging or polyamory, the common theme is that the culture they establish is a matriarchal one. The purpose is to create a sub-culture where normal sexual mores are removed and replaced with a shame-free environment, where the normal covert desire for opportunistic extra-pair-copulations, is allowed to become an overt one.

This creates an artificial suspension of the normal rules of the sexual marketplace, with no Sex Rank penalties for "being a slut" and the ability given to women to spread getting their Alpha and Beta needs met over multiple men rather than just one. They can take Alpha from one or more men and Beta from others. As a result there is near zero resistance to the female sexual hypergamy impulse.

Therefore as a man, your primary goal is to be clearly hotter than the other men also participating in this. Ideally you should be the very hottest man in your sub-cultural group.

The second thing is to be become adept at convincing the less attractive men that experiencing jealousy is a natural reaction, but one they have to work through as a personal growth issue, until they find enjoyment in passively accepting you having sex with their love interest.

The third thing is to convince the less attractive men that the right of females to choose their sexual partners in the sub-culture is of vital importance. If other females do not choose them, it's just perfectly fine and while experiencing anger is a natural reaction, they should work through this as a personal growth issue until they find enjoyment in passively accepting you having sex with their love interest.

The fourth thing is to convince the less attractive men that no one owns another person and you can't really control anyone. So if their love interest decides to end their relationship and move in with you, there was nothing they could have really done to stop it, inevitably she was going to leave at some point. If it wasn't going to be you, it was going to be someone else. So while experiencing sadness at the loss of their love interest is a natural reaction, they should work through this as a personal growth issue until they find enjoyment in passively accepting you having sex with their love interest.

Also it's helpful to have a really big penis.

The rest of the details about non-monogamy are just everyone's Rationalization Hamsters having a press conference.

70 - Be Playfully Mean To Girls Because They Like It

February 22, 2011

I remember a common occurrence in my younger years - seeing an endless variant on boys being playfully mean to girls and having the girls squealing in outrage. Buckets of water tossed on them. Icky spiders tossed on them. Mud flicked at them. On and on and on. It was always something thrown at them that they didn't want.

I was always appalled because that's not a very nice way to act. On rare occasion I might say something about it and tell the boys off and tell them to stop being mean, or offer the girls my towel to dry off or whatever. I also struggled to date. No correct that. I couldn't buy a date with a suitcase of money, my parents' booze and a limo. Even worse was that frequently...no correct that...even worse was that all the time, the sunbathing girl that got a bucket of water tossed on her started going out with the guy that threw the water.

You treat girls well and they ignore you. You treat girls bad and they want you. That makes no sense. Is the world broken?

So anyway, somehow I got out of the horrible years of teen angst and I stumbled onto a killer technique of getting dates. I would walk in the direction of a girl I was interested in, stand near her for approximately four months to attract her attention and then try not to vomit as I asked her out.

Thanks to the two girls for every guy sex ratio imbalance in the Christian community I was in, I had fabulous success with this method. Over the first year and a bit of dating I smoothed out the kinks and got the standing next to the target down to two months. Just as I got my stuff really together, I met Jennifer and played a devastating aloof game by not kissing her and leaving her country as soon as I met her. She folded baby, she folded.

So anyway, it's just so nice to be married and not have to run around trying to date and meet people. Plus I'm with someone that likes me for me. The world seems right in that I can do something nice for her and she doesn't start gazing off into the distance like she's wondering where she is and how she got here.

We had yet more snow fall yesterday - just a few inches - and I was out shoveling the driveway when Jennifer came home. I stopped shoveling for a moment and walked to the garage door and lifted it up for her, so she could just drive in without having to get out and do it herself. It only took half a minute, but it was nice. She stopped for a second and put the passenger side window down and yelled through it, "Thank you! I love you!"

Which was my cue to toss a shovelful of snow at her through the open window of her car. I just roared with laughter as she squealed inside the car with arms failing about like she was fighting off a bee. Once out of the car she scooped snow out while playfully yelling at me, "You're EVIL!" I just laughed some more and kept shoveling. Later that night I made her squeal twice more.

71 - How A Bad MMF Leads To Polyamory Weakly

February 24, 2011

From Polyamory Weekly: "After losing his wife to his best friend and acknowledging he is comfortable with swinging, Tony asks if he should be poly."

At first I just laughed out loud - he couldn't even handle a relationship with one woman, how is he capable of handling a relationship with more than one woman? No don't do that, you just can't handle it.

I never got around to posting on it, but it stuck in my head. Now that I'm looking at it again, it looks a little different.

He's very likely done some sort of swinging with his wife or MMF (threesome with 2 male and 1 female) with his best friend involved and that all went boom in his face. It's usually a big hit to your Alpha to allow your wife to have sex with another man, and a big Alpha boost to the guy that gets to play the walk on stud role. If all three of them: the husband, the wife and the best friend were objectively 7s, the dynamic of doing an MMF means the husband turns into a 5 or 6, the wife stays a 7 and the best friend turns into an 8 or 9. So the natural risk to that dynamic is that the wife is going to jump ship from one man to the other.

It's a horribly risky thing for the husband in that if everything goes well, he has a couple of great sexual sessions, but if it goes bad he gets stripped of his wife and possibly gets hammered on the house / child support / alimony / assets front as well. The wife risks nothing and gets great sexual sessions and maybe a new man. The best friend risks nothing, gets great sexual sessions and can win the wife and whatever assets come with her. This is why wives that are risked in this ridiculous bargain view their husbands with less respect for the sheer idiocy of it all. With less respect comes less attraction and thus the Sex Rank hit. The best friend gains Sex Rank in her eyes because he's obviously smart enough to see a good thing and women are turned on by the ruthlessness of a predatory male.

For the wife, it's very predictable that she would seriously consider switching men. This switching is not an accidental side effect, it is the intended effect. She's trying the best friend out for size as a test drive. If she likes him better, she's making her move.

When the best friend agreed to have sex with his wife, he probably did it with the intentional purpose of stealing her. Pretty much all he has to do is when he's on top of her, pump extra hard and quietly whisper into her ear that he would never share her like this and she deserves better.

So anyway... back to the story...

The dude loses his wife to his best friend, but he's still turned on by the memories of her being banged right in front of him, so multiple-partner sex and relationships still excite him. So obviously he's still interested in swinging, but there's just one little problem - he doesn't have a wife anymore, so he can't even buy his way into swinging.

So, um... can't be cuckolded anymore, can't swing... so all that's left as an option is polyamory.

Then I realize what he's really thinking. He's not even expecting more than one woman; he's trying to get back up to half a woman. Maybe just a third of a woman. He's sex and relationship bankrupt. So sure, why not order from the dollar menu.

72 - Jennifer Answers Some Questions

February 28, 2011

Do you guys really have sex every day? Is that even possible?

I know, right?! It is possible! It is a rare thing for us to not do "something" every day...and it doesn't have to be full on intercourse to count as "something." A hand job, a blow job, a massage with benefits...we're still having that time of closeness and connection to each other at the end of the day. We do have actual intercourse more often than anything else, but frankly sometimes the girly parts need a night off and I'm happy to cater to what Athol wants.

How do you keep Athol interested in you sexually? He seems, um... intense?

Yep, intense is a good word to use. It helps that he's just so interested in sex in general, and I'm the go-to girl! We have had times where we've had "the talk" about me stepping it up in one way or another, and I do my best to listen to suggestions and go along with enthusiasm. I have to consciously think about mixing it up sometimes because I'm so happy with anything that happens...I have to remember that he needs more variety and intensity than I do sometimes.

How do you feel about everything being on the Internet about your sex life?

I like that I get editorial power before anything gets posted. It also helps that I will never actually meet most of his readers face to face. There are a very few times that I have asked him to edit more racy paragraphs down to something that doesn't make me blush, and he respects my privacy in that way. That all being said, I'm not running around my office at work saying, "Hey guys, did you read last night's post about what a fabulous weekend I had banging my husband?!" I believe very strongly that he has good things to say that can help people and that if using examples from our life helps someone, then it's all good.

Are you really okay with the male dominance thing? Why?

I am okay with the male dominance thing as described by Athol...which is to say that male dominance does not mean that I don't have a brain, or don't have the ability to manage my own life or my children's lives...just that I like him to take the lead in some things. The word dominance can have some negative connotations...the way we live it there are no negative connotations- we're not talking chains and disrespect, we're talking someone being the natural leader and someone being the natural follower. When the situation calls for it I'm perfectly capable of being the leader and can enjoy it to a point, but especially in our sex life I'm more of a natural follower.

I'm a little embarrassed to say this, but as a woman I'm slightly worried about Jennifer's enjoyment of the sex... I am worried about the framing of the sex in this post like it's a job for Jennifer and no sex as a "night off."

Athol just told me, "You have to go read the comments...people are worried about you!" Thank you for your concern, but maybe you're misunderstanding the tone of me having a "night off." This is just our catch phrase, not me feeling like sex is my wifely "job." (Easier to talk about it in front of the kiddies if you can use the phrase "night off" and know what the other person means.) True, our default setting is "yes, sex please", but that's the default for both of us. I enjoy our sex life, and if I'm not in the mood for something he doesn't push me. Also, not every night is blog-worthy...sometimes it's just "a quickie" and that's okay. He will initiate and suggest, but not push. It's no fun to have sex with someone who isn't into it.

Do you worry that Athol is going to cheat on you? Dump you for a younger hotter someone? Doesn't him knowing all this stuff make you nervous?

I have very few insecurities as far as Athol cheating on me or leaving me. I know that there is never a 100% guarantee for any human being, but it comes down to trust. I trust that he is going to "use his powers for good" so to speak. He didn't delve into this area of research and writing in order to find a way to cheat on me or dump me, he did it in order to understand marriage better, and to make our marriage better. He doesn't go around hitting on other women randomly, and his friendly, occasionally flirtatious nature is one of the things I enjoy about him. Besides, he knows I'd kick his butt if he tried to leave (okay, so maybe I'd have my hired goon kick his butt...).

Athol - Actually I think Jennifer is being generous on the final question. I obviously have a very high sex drive and struggle with fidelity at times in a general sense, so my research into the subject wasn't from a perfectly saintly perspective. However, I do look into everything and the aftermath of cheating is utterly appalling; Jennifer simply doesn't deserve that and I cannot say she hasn't made herself available to me. If not "banging everyone" is a cost of being married to her, it's a cost I'm okay with. We do have an ongoing sexual imbalance, but she's doing her part, so what remains is my problem to deal with. In no small part, the purpose of the blog is to give me an outlet for some of my excess sexual energy. Marriage is about reality and I know I have more than a good thing in her. She trusts me more than I trust myself and I want to live up to that. If I lost her from my own stupidity, I doubt I would ever stop mourning.

73 - The Highlight Reel Isn't Magic

March 2, 2011

When I was 10 or 11, I read "The Hite Report", my first book about sex.

I didn't have a single date in high school.

When I was 18 I met this fabulous girl, she was 14, so I passed.

The same thing happened a few months later with a different girl.

I didn't have a single date in my first year of college.

My best friend asked a girl I desperately wanted out before I did.

I watched them date for a year before they split, she wouldn't date me then because "it would be awkward."

When I was 18, she was 30. She said it would have been easy to let me, but she didn't.

My best friend did it again with another girl I liked before I finally realized he wasn't my friend.

When I was 19, it took a month to ask my first real girlfriend out.

My relationship lasted three months.

It took eighteen months for the grief to end afterwards.

When I was 20, she was 26 and my second real girlfriend. It was just a bad mistake to have gotten involved.

I've had special relationships last for: one month, three weeks, two weeks, a week and just a single day.

For several years the girl I really loved and wanted was anorexic, so I purposely didn't ask her out.

She had three boyfriends during that time, I didn't hate them, but it hurt anyway.

I met Jennifer when I was 21.

For three years I lived in New Zealand, she lived in America.

We saw each other on vacations at Christmas twice.

When I was 24 I lost my virginity to Jennifer.

Two weeks later we got married.

When I was 25 I lost my faith in God and my justification for waiting so long for sex.

I was angry. So very, very angry.

I started nursing school.

When I was 26 we had our first daughter.

We nearly lost our house.

I finished nursing school.

When I was 27 we had our miscarriage.

Jennifer got pregnant again, but the last five months she was very high risk. We had to stop sex until after she had recovered from the birth.

When I was 28 we had our second daughter.

When I was 29 we flirted with swinging, I wanted it; she wanted me. I shut up about it.

The book I had started writing on swinging is in a big dusty folder.

When I was 30 I made big plans. None of them happened. I think and read about everything.

When I was 31, her mammogram said "probably malignant."

She sobbed in my arms every night for two weeks until the biopsy surgery.

It was my job not to cry.

It wasn't cancer, but the pain from the biopsy scars hurt her for three more years.

Our sex had to be quite careful for about a year or it hurt her left breast.

The left breast itself was off limits for at least two years.

When I was 32 I had a serious emotional connection develop with a female friend.

She made herself known as available.

The friendship ended because I wouldn't make a move on her.

When I was 33 nothing much happened.

When I was 34 nothing much happened.

When I was 35 I started experimenting with dominance on Jennifer.

She reacted positively; I still struggled with it, but continued anyway. Slowly.

When I was 36 I quit nursing and went into real estate.

When I was 37 I should have quit real estate.

When I was 38 I went back to nursing.

When I was 39 Jennifer had another bad mammogram.

This time I cried. I hid that from her.

She was okay, the biopsy recovery was just as few weeks.

I purposely developed a close relationship with someone just to see if I could do it.

I could. I had no plan after that.

I unconsciously leveraged the other relationship for more intense sex from Jennifer.

Jennifer agreed, I broke off the other relationship.

Despite no sex with her, I was emotionally hooked in.

Breaking it off took over a year.

I discovered there is also a male rationalization hamster. It's humbling.

I am truly sorry for that relationship.

When I was 40 my father died.

I came to terms with monogamy.

I told Jennifer she was right about the swinging and apologized.

I finally started to enjoy being dominant over Jennifer.

Jennifer has been in love with me the whole time. I'm awed by that.

I have sucked in information my whole life.

I have read about sex and relationships since I was 10 or 11.

I have read hundreds of books on sex

I have read thousands of articles on sex.

I have read tens of thousands of blog posts on sex.

I've watched my share of porn.

I've worked almost exclusively with women for fifteen years.

At first I just blended in with them all.

I can't anymore - I'm a man.

I have never been able to silence my thinking and struggle to understand sex and relationships.

I know I don't know it all, but now I finally know enough. No more theory, just the killer app.

I started reversing the flow of information.

I have written hundreds of posts.

I have answered thousands of emails.

I've heard hundreds upon hundreds of stories of other people's marriages.

I've been told the most intimate details of other's lives.

I've had to tell some men that they were too late, she was already cheating .

I feel guilty for taking so long to get my ideas out there.

I'm sorry if what I knew could have saved you from divorce, but I took too long to say it.

I have friends, followers and fans. I am truly flattered by this. I am proud of the blog.

The book is almost finished and it seems as if my whole life has been working towards this.

I have craved sex for as long as I can remember.

My bad luck with women before her, is good luck in retrospect.

I have had clear temptations and struggles, but I keep returning to her.

She is still my only and I am hers.

It matters, if only to us.

When we married, I was like a dam breaking into her.

We never actually counted how often we have had sex, but it's around 5000 times in sixteen years.

We never planned to rack up a number, each night was its own night.

By definition, half of our sex was below average.

Only 30% of what we tried sexually worked for us.

Hardly any of our sex would make the highlight reel. But there is a highlight reel.

I am the lightning, but she is the earth.

So if you see a fabulous blog, a clever theory in a book, a man that understands women, a devoted wife, a happy marriage and ridiculously good sex life - understand that it's all true, it's just that we didn't unwrap all this on a Christmas morning in 1991. What we have is good, but it is not impossible. We are a special couple, but at the same time, all that we've done to achieve that is the ordinary.

Our path may not be your path, but you can make choices on your path too. You can do this too. So stop talking about it. Do something about it. The highlight reel isn't magic.

74 - Female Hypergamy is Rational

March 19, 2011

If a female 7 can get pregnant to a male 9 or 10, it's rational for her to do so. Marrying a 7 will never accomplish a result as potentially good as what five minutes with a 9 or 10 can do. A single sexy son can trump three plain looking kids for passing on her genes. If she can pass it off as the 7's kid, or convince him to be a stepfather, then that's even better. She can have a sexy son and two plain looking kids.

If a female 7 is married to a male who has slumped to a 6, and a male 8 shows her serious interest...it's rational for her to leave the 6 and attach herself to the 8.

Half the work Rationalization Hamsters do is to convince women not to cheat on or dump the man they're currently with. Most moralizing is done to work against the rational purpose of benefiting the individual, with a view to improving the collective good. So most of the time the Rationalization Hamster is telling her to be a good girl even though she probably would rather have more fun being a little bad.

But when actually presented with a perfect opportunity to get away with something truly critical though, the Rationalization Hamster has to quickly unpick all that prior bullshit and make up some new bullshit to convince her to actually do something, well... rational; like get pregnant to a 10 or trade up 2 Sex Rank points in a divorce and remarriage gambit.

There is a nice upside to Female Hypergamy though. If you increase your Sex Rank, it's rational that your wife wants to have sex with you more. So get to it.

75 - If She Offers You A Free Cookie – Take The Cookie

March 27, 2011

I've asked for some questions from the ladies and got essentially the same question twice and it's really an easily fixable one.

Anonymous said...

"How can I explain that I don't always need to have an orgasm during sex? Sometimes it really is ok for him to get off without me. The constant pressure to orgasm is taking the fun out of our sex life."

Anonymous said...

"I second the "I don't have to orgasm all the time" idea. I get it that he gets off by it, it boosts the ego, etc. But sometimes I *do* want to focus on his orgasm! I get the same enjoyment he does by experiencing my partner's joy!"

I think it's really a combo of two things. (1) Him being programmed to believe that he's being a bad guy if he has an orgasm and you don't and (2) he's confused as to why you aren't into him enough to want an orgasm. So it's all a heavy duty Beta mindset for him.

The solution is to simply take what the woman says about wanting an orgasm at face value. If she wants one, then co-create it with her. If she doesn't want an orgasm and is offering herself for sex, then just use her for your own needs and don't care about it beyond that. It's a far more Alpha approach and essentially boils down to a marital version of a pump and dump. If she's offering her body to you and wants nothing in return for it, just take the free cookie and move on with your day.

That sounds like it's offensively rude, but she's the one offering it and when you don't take advantage of it, it's a disappointment to her... or you essentially push her into a sex act she doesn't really want to do. Oh hang on... that sounds a little... ahhh... rapey doesn't it? Awkward.

I mean I'm all for rough sex, spanking her ass, calling her dirty names and cumming on her face and everything, all of which can look horribly offensive... but if she's smiling and giving the thumbs up consent, then it's all good. I'm an asshole in the bedroom, but I am a consensual asshole.

But if you're being sweet, kind, polite and then blatantly ignore her request not to orgasm and strong-arm her into having one using the weight of your relationship as leverage, well that all looks very charming from the outside. You're a nice man attentive to her sexual needs, but you're ignoring the consent issue. So you can be a very nice man in the bedroom, but non-consensually nice.

For the husband, the solution is easy - just take the free cookie and use her like the personal fuck toy she's asking you to treat her as. It's about as much fun as trying to get a cat in a cat carrier for a vet appointment as trying to get a woman to orgasm when she doesn't really want to. If the pussy doesn't want it, you really have to end up forcing the issue to get the job finished. The pussy is usually relieved that the shoving is over once it's done, but that's not the same as actually being happy with what happened. So take the easy route, just pound her for a bit and have your orgasm, kiss her, give her a little cuddle and then move on with your day. Women quite like this treatment from their men (if only once in a while), plus she's even directly asking you to do this to her.

For the women reading, the solution is also fairly easy - stop complaining about this sort of sex (talking) and stop tolerating having this sort of sex (action). If you nag at him, or whine or even politely say that you don't want an orgasm, but then you passively allow him to push you into having one, you are in fact tolerating the entire thing and creating the environment where he thinks you actually really want an orgasm, but just need to be pushed into having one. So the actual message you are sending him by your actions is that you want an orgasm.

So you should be verbally clear early on in the piece that you're offering yourself for his sexual needs, but you don't want an orgasm yourself. If he starts trying to obviously get you off, then you need to stop him. Physically push his hands/head/whatever off/away from your vagina and explain in a clear firm tone of voice, "I'm not having an orgasm right now, I'm happy if you have one."

If he doesn't get it and he attempts to escalate you towards an orgasm for a second time, repeat the first stopping effort, but with the additional step of physically getting up out of the bed and standing next to it. Only get back into the bed if he can verbalize understanding that he can have an orgasm, but that you don't want one. (This is probably the moment where he "gets it.")

If he tries to escalate you again after that, then just stop the sex completely for the night. Then just frame it as that he needs to go do whatever it is that he needs to do - masturbate, sleep on the couch, have a cold shower or whatever it is to finish off his day - and tomorrow is a new day and you'll take it from there; but we are all done for tonight. You're probably pissed off by this point and rightfully so.

If he actually gets it and you have sex together and he comes and you don't, then reward him afterwards (action) and make it clear that despite not having an orgasm, you really enjoyed the experience. The easy way to do this is to simply cuddle up to him afterwards, head on his shoulder, pressed up against him, bonus points for lightly fondling his balls. Tell him you love him. Or try this line..."I love it when you make me feel like a woman."

Which is a backdoor way of telling him you love it when he acts like a man.

So just to recap - if she wants an orgasm, then you should co-create it together and do whatever it takes to make it happen. If she doesn't want an orgasm and is okay with him having one, he should take the easy dunk. I mean we work so hard to get a wife to hand out free cookies....

76 - The Red Pill, The Nookie and The Best Revenge

March 28, 2011

The guys writing about Game on the Internet, including myself, all have a starkly pragmatic Red Pill way of looking at the world and women. The difference between us and the character of Neo in The Matrix, is that we weren't offered a clear choice of taking the Red Pill or not. The Red Pill was given to us via personal horror: walk-away wives, girlfriends leaving for a guy they said was an asshole, cleaned out bank accounts, "it's not your baby", no sex for months or years on end, the slow transformation of your darling bride into a venomous screechtard.

In my case, I've been lucky as to how I was given the Red Pill. I got a good dose of it early on in my teen years when the major fallout from it was not much more than hurt feelings. A lot of what is good about Jennifer and myself is a result of that, but there's been unwittingly good luck as well. A lot of what I've been doing with my writing is attempting to reverse engineer that luck, so that everyone else can use some of it too.

I suspect that for most guys, learning Game was Plan B. Plan A was taking the Blue Pill and being with one special girl forever. It just didn't work out so well.

The real challenge of taking the Red Pill though, is learning to forgive her for whatever it was that she did to you. You don't have to forget, it's not even possible to forget something, but it is possible to forgive her. She probably already moved on mentally from you long ago, so it's for your benefit I suggest you forgive and move on. I don't mean you try and get her back or save her from whatever happened either. Her choices are hers to live with.

Getting the nookie is all fun and good, I get that. The nookie is very important and a big piece of your personal puzzle of happiness. But life is a long road to be angry at someone, plus there's only so much room for emotion inside you. If you're still deeply angry, or hurt, or hating, then there's less room inside you for happiness, joy and love. If the purpose of Game is not to actually be happy, then why are you doing it? Revenge?

It's fine to be mad about things. It's normal and expected that you're mad about shit that went down. At some point you just got to run with Plan B though. There's nothing about the Red Pill that says you can't make a change in the way you do things, readjust and have a better life. If you've already taken the Red Pill, you've already started to change anyway, the only question is to what degree and how far you take it.

If you want revenge, know that living well is the best revenge and living well involves happiness, joy and love.

Though when word gets out that you are "living well", should she ever comes back trying to re-instigate herself into your life, the look on her face when you tell her she's had her chance is probably going to be pretty satisfying too. There's a Red Pill for chicks as well.

77 - Temptation

March 29, 2011

Jennifer and I had a Date Night on Saturday, so we had an adult movie from the secret sock drawer and some regular rented DVDs as well. I went to return them tonight before we got charged for an extra night.

Jennifer (smirking): "It would be funny if you accidently returned the wrong movies."

Me: "Ah... we rented them with your credit card."

Jennifer: "Oh, well never mind then."

...

Jennifer: "Do I want to know what you're thinking?"

Me: "Well, now I'm tempted..."

78 - Her Needs For Stimulation And Relationship Engagement

March 30, 2011

Reader Question: I'm curious what your thoughts are on women and drama. Some Game blogs proclaim that women "need" drama and woe is the husband/player who doesn't feed them a steady diet of faux crises and kerfuffles. If you don't, they say, women will make up their own dramatic crises and rope you in. Seems very similar to shit-testing but I haven't figured it out yet.

Also, your blog came along too late to help me save my marriage, but I use your stuff all the time. I'm amazed how well it (usually) works. I can't believe how much easier acquiring vagina has become.

Finally, I'll buy the book to show my support for you but I won't read it in public! Sorry!

Athol: Hi there, yes and no...

Think of it as women (and men too) needing a certain level of stimulation to feel engaged in the relationship with the other. Some women need more, some women need less. There's usually a fairly good correlation between extroversion and needing high stimulation and introversion and needing low stimulation.

If you have too high of a stimulation - say a shy wallflower matched up with crazy drug using biker guy, they tend to freak out and withdraw from the guy. He's simply too high stimulation. They aren't comfortable with him. Not enough

Beta too much Alpha. Or they try and calm him down and Betaize him some.

If you have too low of a stimulation - party princess thinking about being a stripper matched with science geek nice guy, they start getting very bored and under-stimulated by him. Not enough Alpha, too much Beta. They might just leave and find someone more fun / exciting / stimulating. The other thing they can do though is subconsciously create some sort of relationship drama to create the stimulation they need to feel engaged in the relationship.

For the most part though, the better the male calibrates to the females needs for stimulation, the less likely she is to create relationship drama. You having to make up "reverse shit tests" to engage her is a failure of sorts showing that you haven't maintained things. For the most part all you need to do to make a woman feel engaged in the relationship is: kiss her properly, fuck her hard, be playfully instigating with her, listen to her and not endlessly do the same shit over and over like always going to the same place to eat. Just mix it up a bit.

Some couples have an excellent match on stimulation and sail easily along, but usually one half of the couple is higher stimulation than the other. For Jennifer and myself, I am the high stimulation half of the couple and she is lower. Jennifer simply has no time to even think about testing me with everyday drama because she's trying to keep up with my all purpose horniness and ADHD. Half the reason I write the blog is just to be a huge stimulation thing for me and a mental energy sink. We've also figured this out as a couple and Jennifer responds well to my demands to be stimulated, though she tends not to think of me needing something as much as I do, because she herself doesn't need that level of stimulation.

The problem when the female is the higher stimulation partner, is that very often women have a deep need to be sexually responsive to a man. So they need to be able to "just sit there" and have him make the moves that they respond too. So when a high stimulation woman who needs to be sexually responsive is matched with a lower stimulation man, he just doesn't playfully "mess with her" enough. So in order to both keep her frame as being sexually responsive to him, and get stimulation, she can't just come out and say "hey I need you to mess with me a bit because I'm under-stimulated." So she has to force the issue by creating some other drama that forces the man to engage with her. All this is usually quite unconscious on her part.

The solution for the lower stimulation male, matched with a higher stimulation female, is to be more conscious about instigating things with her. That's easy enough to do with the Ten Second Kisses, texting her frequently, teasing her a lot and so on. Plus it's a more conscious thought process that "I may not care that I am having a cheeseburger every time we go out to eat, but she gets bored of the same places over and over." You can do highly stimulating things with her - ride the roller coasters, see a scary movie, go para-sailing, travel, etc. Also you can direct her and suggest tasks for her - it's a way of being responsive to you and it's something to do. Those tasks can be sexual and non-sexual in nature. "I need a couple new shirts, can you help me shop for some?" "I want to see you with a shaved pussy tonight." "Stockings and a top of your choice tonight please." Then when she complies and does stuff with/for you, thank her.

So it's not really a case of having to dream up crises for her, just playfully mess with her and don't be boring. If she needs more stimulation, get her to do something for you and say thanks. All she's usually trying to do is feel engaged in the relationship.

As an aside, this is very closely related to Fitness Testing. A high stimulation woman can create drama that essentially is a Fitness Test and you do have to pass it as a Fitness Test. But the cause of the testing lies in her stimulation needs. You can end up facing Fitness Test after Fitness Test if you can't stimulate her enough to feel engaged in the relationship. Sometimes though, a Fitness Test is just something she throws at you to see if she can get away with behaving badly and unrelated to a stimulation need. There's a difference between being bored and a bitch.

There we go. Hope that answers the question.

Pity you can't read the book in public... maybe I do need a special version with a cover that has a picture of a duck wearing a little yellow rain hat.

79 - Girl Game: Have Long Hair

April 5, 2011

Long hair is a marker for physical good health, is a feminine appearance marker and the overwhelming majority of men are attracted to long hair. Most husbands react to their wives lopping all their hair into some sort of short pixie cut quite badly. Kinda the same way you would react if he suddenly announced he'd shortened his cock to two inches long. You're not going to really say anything, just make that strangling sound in your throat and hope that it can eventually grow back.

And yes I know, long hair is more work to take care of. Yes I know washing baby puke out of your hair is disgusting. Yes I know having a toddler deciding to latch onto your hair and rappel down the back of the couch is annoying.

Men really like it though. Shoulder length is just fine, anything past your mid-back starts seeming to be a little long. No need to go Rapuzel on us.

Dozens of times in my life I've experienced having one of those mild background crush feelings for a woman, instantly disappear as soon as she cuts her hair very short. I mean seriously, real feelings of attraction just instantly gone. Monday I was into you with your pretty shoulder length hair; Tuesday morning arrived and you walked in with it trimmed away to not all that much and I have no more attraction to you.

Of course all her friends and coworkers just love her new hair style! Of course they would, she just botched her appearance and if she falls off the top of the sexy ladder, everyone else gets to move up a place. So like OMG I just love it!

Some men even are more attracted to a particular hair color. I'm a blonde guy. One of the serious attraction points Jennifer had to me when I met her was her wonderful blonde hair. By "wonderful blonde hair" I mean badly-damaged-with-an-accidental-bleaching-incident when I met her, but wow I loved it. She's actually brunette, which to me is "meh whatever."

In the middle of last year she actually reverted back to her natural hair color by dying it back that way. She liked it, all her friends and coworkers just loved it, loved it, loved it. Me... "meh whatever." Jennifer with blonde hair is a solid 9 to me. Jennifer with whatever that crap her natural hair color was is a 7 or maybe 8 to me. I can't help myself feeling that change in emotion. I'm not going to divorce her for being brunette, I'm just going to be less into her.

I didn't make a stink or anything, I actually tried hard to not be bothered by it or complain about it. I don't think I said anything about it, but a few months back all the blonde highlighting mysteriously returned. The little boost of my attraction returned as well. Attraction is not controllable.

The other easy move with long hair is the classic girlish pony tail. Probably not something to wear to the office if you're out of the twenties-and-single cohort, but there's no reason why you can just sweep it up like that on the weekend once in a while. You can be 52 and rock a pony tail around the house on a Saturday morning. It's a strong "look I'm a girl" statement. Seriously, why not try it? Mess with him a bit, tease him a little and then just swish your pony tail into the distance with an over the shoulder look like you used to....

80 - Girl Game: Find Out What Turns Him On

April 6, 2011

Some things basically attract all men: nice skin, nice hair, nice eyes, nice boobs, and nice butt yada yada yada. You do what you can with that of course, but you can't exactly spin a cocoon around yourself and suddenly bust out in six weeks like a magical tits-and-ass-butterfly either. What you really want is something easy and practical to score some easy points in the attraction department.

Well sometimes those things really do exist as there's often some sort of accessories or clothes that turn your man on in particular. So they work for him, but not all men. He's not always going to tell you about them as some of these things can be deeply personal veins of erotic kink for him. He may or may not understand why he feels as he does about them either.

So you're going to have to ask him about what things turn him on, or he may have already told you some of them and you've ignored them. Once you get it into your head to do them, they are always automatic +1 attraction when you do them. You don't even need to understand these things and often they can seem to most people to be decidedly mundane. You initial reaction is quite possibly going to be confusion rather than icky repulsion.

Some of my own personal kink follows...

Big hoop-like gold earrings - I will always absolutely zone out and stare at them. Always an automatic +1 on any woman wearing them. This one I know is related to my first serious girlfriend Mary wearing a lot of big hoop-like gold earrings as part of her overall look. The experience of feeling intense attraction somehow got anchored into these damn earrings. It's not like I even drift off and start remembering Mary either, it's just a +1 associated with that sort of earrings. (You would think that Jennifer would have a small collection of these, but she doesn't. I don't know why either, I've mentioned it on several occasions, but don't want to mention it again because things are going so well right now between us. Jennifer adds: DOH! Must buy big hoopy earrings...)

Blonde Hair - I mentioned that yesterday. Blonde hair is always +1 for me. That's not wildly uncommon, it's just there. Why this one is, I'm not 100% sure, but that's probably another attraction anchoring thing from my endless elementary and middle school days crush on Kristen who had... blonde hair.

Sundresses - I do like dresses in a general sense, but sundresses just do me in. Not sure exactly why this one is for me. Awkward relationship friendship girl Rebecca wore a lot of these, but I think it might predate her a little, but that probably anchored the interest further.

Actually the sundress thing is a perfect example of where when he reveals "look these really turn me on" and you just go "Huh?" at him. You're expecting him to say something like "I want to see you wearing nothing but a G-String tuned to A", and instead you think you heard him mumble something about sundresses.

Jennifer was wearing a blue and white dress the day I met her. I can't remember her wedding dress unless I look at a photo. I do remember that blue and white dress though. Even though she couldn't wear it anymore post-pregnancies, when she threw it out during a spring cleaning I was pissed off about it, which surprised both of us lol.

Stockings - No idea on cause. Just OMG hot.

The deepest one though is just ridiculously simple. It's the color pink. I get transfixed by something as simple as a $10 pink T-shirt. That's seriously a +2 for me. I have no idea why that is. Just no idea at all. I never had a girlfriend that wore pink anything in particular, I can't even remember a particular crush that layered up the pink.

If the 80's could come back and that shocking hot pink lipstick could just return to stores everywhere I would be eternally grateful. We've found some shades close and I'm happy enough with them.

As you can see, most of those items are not all that hard to find or wear. It's a certain type of earring. A few blonde highlights. A dress once in a while. Wearing stockings to bed once in a while. A handful of pink shirts and lipstick once in a while. These are things that work for me in particular rather than all men, and Jennifer using them is only mildly inconvenient at worst to her, but she gets a big payoff in my interest in her. Sometimes it's even easier that what you think would work better... a comfy pink sleep shirt beats $100 of lingerie for me.

Well... unless it's pink and black lingerie.

So ask him what turns him on in particular. Then all you have to do is work it into your clothing rotation and you're good to go. Not every single day, just in the rotation. Though I do warn you, if you ask him and he clearly communicates to you something that is cheap, easy and non-offensive to do...

...failing to follow through on that will probably backfire on you quite impressively. The bigger the turn on it is, the bigger the shit-storm you will have created. Don't fuck with people's kink.

81 - Girl Game: Initiate Sex By Touching Him On The Penis

April 8, 2011

One of the most frequent complaints from men is that their wives don't initiate sex with them. In fact they can get pretty tore up about it because they feel sexually rejected by their wives because of it. After being the one to initiate sex for the 100th time, it's easy to start to feel like the other person isn't really all that interested in you. Which is an easy jump to...

"Fuck this shit. I'm just going to see how long it takes for her to initiate sex with me just one time."

Then the sexual drought starts with him pissed off at her, and her wondering why her husband doesn't feel interested in her anymore and is always mad. Could be a while until the 101st time....

I've told the guys to just get the hell over their wives not initiating, and just ask for sex and get things started anyway. For the most part women are sexually responsive to men, so most women just wait to be asked to have sex. So the husband's problem boils down to the fact that they want their wife to act like... well, act like a guy when it comes down to getting sex started.

Generally women do choose to show subtle availability signals though, but generally the husband just misses them completely. Her cooking his favorite food for dinner, having a long hot bath (to be perfectly fresh) and rubbing his upper back slowly for ten seconds while he is distracted with World of Warcraft, just doesn't work very well at letting him know she is in the mood.

Oh sure some nights she could do all that and he will have sex with her, but her "moves" didn't change the outcome because he doesn't understand the subtle approach. He probably still thinks that he initiated sex even though she threw out half a dozen little signals of interest.

See when your husband initiates sex, he usually directly asks for sex, or starts groping you. So when he says/thinks "She never initiates sex." what he really means is "She never just starts touching me on the penis without me asking her to."

So the solution is pretty simple. Once in a while, just start touching him on the penis.

After you initiate sex by touching him on the penis, you can either stay more in control or less in control of the sex as you both like. But after the sex finishes, you should cuddle up to him and say something like, "I got good wife points for initiating right?" and when he agrees, you snuggle in a little more and give yourself a little verbal hi-five. "Yes!"

You can also do the touching him on the penis thing, right through his clothes. Just put your hand out into the front of his pants and feel around for something that feels like a penis. Once you find his penis, rub in an up-down motion gently - and this is important ladies so pay attention - rub in an up-down motion *right on his penis.*

You can also rub your ass all over the area proximal to the penis. Strippers make lots of money doing this, so by you doing this you're actually saving money in the weekly budget too. So that's double good wife points right there. You rock!

82 - Girl Game: Give Him A Fair Warning

April 14, 2011

A comment by MGirl on an earlier post.

MGirl: Anon-I had the same problem with my husband. My sex drive was through the roof, but I was extremely unattracted to him. I suggested he read this blog (he didn't), so I got blunt. I told him I was tired of having to fantasize about other men. I told him I was finding myself looking at other men and wanting them. I told him I wanted sex, but not with him. I wasn't considering, or even threatening cheating, BTW, but I was honest about how I felt. And boy did he perk up then. He started working out regularly, went to go buy new clothing, got his hair cut, and regularly asks me what he can do to increase my attraction to him. My approach was a bit aggressive, maybe, but I was desperate and couldn't see any other option. And it worked!

Athol: This is dead on.

The husband should thank his lucky stars for his choice of wife. Plenty of other women would have simply thrown up their hands and cheated on him or divorced him.

A fair warning is a real gift. But you do have to spell it out clearly and carefully. Asking him to do at least something for creating attraction is a reasonable request.

If you're a husband and you get one of these little talks, or your wife sends you to read here, or hands you my book...that's your sign things need to start changing.

Attraction isn't a choice. As I cover in the Introduction of the Primer, she can't will herself to be attracted to you and have sex with you the way you want her to. But you can will yourself to self improve in ways that will create attraction in her for you.

83 - The Third Wheel

April 16, 2011

I've had three different emails in the last week all dealing with someone starting to attach and just be excessively present with a boyfriend/girlfriend couple. In one case the Third Wheel was female and interested in the boyfriend, in two cases the Third Wheel was male and interested in the girlfriend.

To avoid excessive wordiness and confusion, we'll assume the Third Wheel is male for the rest of the post. But everything applies much the same when it's a female one too.

Generally a persistent Third Wheel male has a keen interest in the girlfriend. His goal is to turn it into a full blown Love Triangle, and then finally completely displace the original boyfriend. The longer the Third Wheel is allowed to stay a Third Wheel, the more traction he gains toward turning it into a Love Triangle. The Third Wheel is very frequently the boyfriends "best friend."

...except that the Third Wheel / Best Friend is completely prepared to leverage anything including his entire friendship, to get the girlfriend for himself. So to be completely blunt, when your best friend is starting to make a play for your girl, the friendship has ended.

Because of basic propinquity, the Third Wheel / Best Friend is probably reasonably attractive to the girlfriend, and the Third Wheel has calculated that he's within Sex Rank striking distance of actually getting the girl. So the longer it goes on, the more her attraction will grow for him. Allowing another guy to hang around your girl endlessly is a weakness display, so that also decreases her attraction to you as well.

At some point the boyfriend is going to get very uncomfortable and pissed off about the whole thing, usually when the girlfriend returns some level of interest to the Third Wheel / Best Friend. Usually it's going to be some small thing she does, she isn't going to jump to sex straight away, it's just going to be something minor like Facebook friending, "popping over to borrow a couple of CD's", an unusual phone call, a bunch of texting or so on. But the boyfriend is going to get the absolute pit-of-the-stomach heebie-jeebies about it.

The next thing that happens, is the boyfriend will say something to the girlfriend about the situation and ask what the hell is going on, knock it off, yada yada yada. She will always firmly deny any interest in the Third Wheel/Best Friend, plus do some sort of dramatic routine of apologizing or outrage at being questioned, with a declaration of interest in only the boyfriend.

It is in no way over. All the boyfriend-girlfriend conversation does is act as an announcement from the boyfriend to the girlfriend that the Third Wheel issue is going to be resolved one way... or the other.

The girlfriend will be paying extreme attention to what the boyfriend does about the Third Wheel over the next short time frame. If the boyfriend essentially gets rid of the Third Wheel, then the situation resolves by the girlfriend becoming more interested in the boyfriend. But if the Third Wheel is allowed to continue to maintain constant contact, it's a terrible weakness display. Very likely the girlfriend will signal her interest to the Third Wheel and it's basically over for the boyfriend from then.

Importantly upping the ante with the girlfriend doesn't work. You busting out an engagement ring doesn't work to fix the Third Wheel problem. Oh she can say "yes" and get distracted for a few weeks, but the problem isn't the male-female relationship, but that the male is weak to another male and allowing access to the female. You getting married with the

Third Wheel as your Best Man is very likely not going to play out well at all.

Once he starts making an aggressive push for your girl, you've already lost the friendship. It's just up to you whether or not you lose the girl as well. And trust me it's going to be unbelievably awful seeing them together and knowing what you could have done.

So practice with me...

"Dude, fuck off, we're on a date."

84 - Jennifer and the Two Hundred Pound Raccoon

April 17, 2011

Jennifer and I usually go grocery shopping together. I used to do it all myself back in my SAHD + working all weekend days, then somehow she took it over for a long time. Now that the kids are old enough to be home alone, we sneak out together on shopping dates.

So anyway, yesterday...

Eggs were on sale. English muffins were on sale. Cheese was crazy on sale. Bacon was crazy on sale plus we had a coupon. See where I'm going with this?

This morning I'm up and awake at about 6:30am. No reason, just up, so I clear the email, plow the feed reader and do about two hours of reading and commenting on Talk About Marriage.

Eventually I become hungry.

Around 10am I check on Jennifer who is awake and still lying in bed and very clearly not cooking me breakfast. So I kiss her and playfully suggest she should be heading to the kitchen. I poke youngest daughter awake for good measure too or she'll never fall asleep tonight.

I have my shower and once done I come back down to the smell of sizzling bacon and the makings of delicious bacon, egg and cheese on toasted English muffins. They are divine; as is she.

There's a lot of leftover bacon though. So I suggest tonight we should have the beef, fresh bread and the salad makings for dinner... with the crumbled bacon in the salad. It's far easier to get your wife to make you dinner if you know what's in the fridge and ask for something actually possible to cook.

Jennifer: "Oh really?"

There's actually a mildly testing tone here, as if to stay, "Dude! I just cooked breakfast for you and now you're ordering dinner?"

Me: "Well we can't just throw the leftover bacon away..."

That does kind of make sense and I just ignored her testing tone.

Me: "... Well. Not without me eating it out of the trash anyway."

She laughs and says "Okay." She can't win a test against me if I make her laugh, so I make her laugh a lot. I tend to act like a raccoon around bacon and if you're ever five feet tall fronting up against a two hundred pound raccoon, it's best to just let the raccoon do whatever it wants to do.

So tonight for dinner we're having grilled beef, fresh bread and a salad with little bits of bacon in it. She'll probably cook, I'll probably make the run out to get the bread. Might shop from the Redbox in the store and come home with a DVD too.

So if you're ever strapped for an idea in the moment, just ask yourself, "What would a two hundred pound raccoon do?" (WWTHPRD?) Then do that. You'd be surprised at how frequently it's on point.

85 - Girl Game: Post-Coital Cuddling

April 23, 2011

After having sex, you snuggling into him and laying your head on his shoulder will frame him as strong, comforting and powerful. It's like you're telling him you feel he's got the Alpha Male thing down.

Making him feel more Alpha, is going to make him act more Alpha. You might like that.

There's often a little bit of a chicken and the egg thing happening here for Jennifer and myself. It's usually after the rougher Alpha poundings that she snuggles into me like this. Usually I tease her just a little for it too.

Me: "Well somebody liked that didn't she."

Jennifer: "Shut up." (Snuggles closer.)

I do utterly adore this position though.

Though the truth is quite often I cuddle up to her after sex... and wake up three to ten minutes later. Just out like a light as I get that hormonal surge after orgasm. Once I wake back up we disengage and then I go back to sleep again. It's actually very difficult for me to fall asleep without having sex. I just lie there... awake.

Jennifer doesn't care of course, she just figures she's topping off the mind control conditioning for another day by having me shoot myself full of vasopressin again. Plus it makes me a terrible candidate for having an affair...

Home wrecking Bitch: "OMG, my husband is coming! Hide!"

Me: (Snores heavily while drooling into pillow)

Other Husband: "WHAT THE HELL IS THIS?!? GET OUT OF BED!!!"

Me: (groggily) "Just five more minutes mom, I promise I'll get up."

See why I avoid that nonsense?

So anyway.... Cuddle up to him in bed after doing it was the point. Also if you do that, all the post-sex drippage ends up on his side of the bed.

86 - Living With A Big Cat

May 8, 2011

Husband losing his wife to another man...

"They have had sex, a lot. She says she likes how he is sexually aggressive with her and enjoys being objectified by him. Admittedly, we have had some tension in this department, but I have tried becoming more aggressive over these last years. We have always enjoyed our sex, but I have always been too gentle and slow I guess. I like to savor her and I have told her this. She appreciates this and enjoys the attention, but it has not been all she wants so I have tried to expand."

Most women like rough sex and being treated like sex objects - if only once in a while. If this is something she wants, and you don't give it to her, you leave the door open to someone else offering it.

I guess what pisses me off is all the public discussion of sex suggests that a man should be gentle and slow in bed. It's just wrong, badly wrong. Sure, the slow and gentle thing once in a while is fine, but not every time.

Psychology Today...

"From 1973 through 2008, nine surveys of women's rape fantasies have been published. They show that about four in 10 women admit having them (31 to 57 percent) with a median frequency of about once a month. Actual prevalence of rape fantasies is probably higher because women may not feel comfortable admitting them.

For the latest report (Bivona, J. and J. Critelli. "The Nature of Women's Rape Fantasies: An Analysis of Prevalence, Frequency, and Contents," Journal of Sex Research (2009) 46:33), psychologists at North Texas University asked 355 college women: How often have you fantasized being overpowered/forced/raped by a man/woman to have oral/vaginal/anal sex against your will?

Sixty-two percent said they'd had at least one such fantasy. But responses varied depending on the terminology used. When asked about being "overpowered by a man," 52 percent said they'd had that fantasy, the situation most typically depicted in women's romance fiction. But when the term was "rape," only 32 percent said they'd had the fantasy. These findings are in the same ballpark as previous reports."

Now quite obviously a rape fantasy is vastly different from rape reality. Actual rape is utterly horrible and evil. But consensual, rough sex can hit the same triggers of enjoyment that the fantasy can.

For Jennifer and myself we really only started discovering it about 4-5 years ago. To be sure we have had rough/firm sex before then, but I was always slightly apologetic about it. And nothing kills the moment faster than asking "Are you okay? I hope I didn't hurt you." right after you finish. Doh!

It was only after reading about it that I really started trying it out on her and to my vast surprise she reacted positively. So I kept throwing it into the mix and she kept liking it. She actually liked it immediately while I struggled with it emotionally for about two years. Seemed a bit aggressive and obnoxious to me, to be honest. I only started enjoying it in the last couple of years.

I'm still growing and learning as I write this blog. About a year ago I tried another experiment. I decided to not just have rough sex with her, but to do it as hard as I could... without regard for her enjoyment or caring about her at all. I mean really, really, really rag doll fuck her like she was rented.

She loved it.

My sweet, kind, gentle, smart, funny, caring, educated, polite, playful, good girl, wife and mother... loved it. Afterwards she melded herself into my side with her head on my shoulder and just purred. The next day she was a little sore in the lady bits, but she texted excitedly back and forth too. She doted on me the next evening.

Cause and effect my love.

Jennifer: This is a "style" of making love that I really enjoy, but that I don't need every day. And thinking about it, part of my positive reaction to the rough stuff is a reaction to his enthusiasm. He is enthusiastically pounding me, therefore I react enthusiastically. The same writhing and moaning might not be quite in keeping with a more sedate encounter.

Athol: It was actually somewhat disturbing to me. Yes I know women aren't mindless robots that have no will power or ability to make choices, but this is a definite influence on wifely behavior. I've seen too many cases of a Nice Guy husband losing out to basically a thuggish lover with not much else going for them.

What I'm saying is, if someone else had screwed Jennifer like that behind my back ten years ago...

...I really don't know if I could have gotten her back. I just don't know.

Don't misunderstand - Jennifer has been a loyal, devoted and honorable wife and I deeply appreciate that about her. But she's a woman nevertheless and like all women, she has an inner slut component to her personality. I'm the one that really gets to see it, but it's there. When I say she has an inner slut, it's a term of respect.

I meet Jennifer when she was 18. She's 38 now... she's grown. Somewhere along the way she stopped being my little "Hello Kitty" virgin and turned into something more akin to a cougar. I mean that in a good way.

The trick with big cats is to feed it the food they like. Otherwise they hunt.

87 - Taken In Hand vs. Captain and First Officer

May 9, 2011

Reader question...

"What is your relationship with the link to Taken In Hand on your blog? Is this something you support? Would you be willing to privately disclose if this is, in fact, the nature of your relationship with Jennifer? Or have you been open about it and I missed it? (No, silly, I haven't been able to read *every* post. Not just yet!)"

This is a more complicated question than you know. For those with the book, I'm going to connect the dots between The Primer Chapters 9 (Captain and First Officer), 11 (Behavior Modification) and 24 (Rough Stuff).

Taken In Hand.com was one of the places that I read heavily and first learned that many women enjoy submission and that male dominance isn't evil in and of itself. I think it's an important resource for that perspective. (It does however seem to be dying a slow death with minimal posting in the last 12 months.)

In terms of us personally, the answer is yes and no. I think the Captain and First Officer model incorporates a fair amount of the Taken In Hand perspective, but without the Domestic Discipline aspect. We do erotic spanking once in a while, but that's quite different.

The Taken In Hand approach with Domestic Discipline essentially is a form of husbandly behavioral management using aversive techniques seeking to stop wifely bad behavior. My approach to behavioral management is to reward good behavior and to purposely not reward bad behavior. A lot of that not rewarding is by reducing attention and allowing the natural consequences for bad behavior take their course.

The trap with Domestic Discipline is if a high stimulation need wife gets her drama fix by a spanking for doing something bad, you are actually reinforcing the bad behavior because she got what she wanted by doing it. If she wants the spanking fix, she has to create a Fitness Test situation to do it. Thus a vicious cycle begins. The spankings can tend to escalate in intensity trying to "break the defiant wife" and after a certain point it all just becomes a senseless beating. I can't imagine doing that to Jennifer and I can't imagine she would stay if I did.

If a couple discovers that the wife (or husband) enjoys the sensation and intensity of being spanked, then you could perceive it as a reward and tie it into their good behavior. I know of a couple where the wife cleans the house from top to bottom in semi-random "cleaning crazies" and gets an erotic spanking as a reward for it. Her husband comes home from work and notices the spic and span... and her sort of bouncing up and down waiting for his attention. He just says "I see" and gives her what she wants that night. It's sort of an inverted Fitness Test this way as he "bumps back" on a clean house. But if she likes it, what's the harm?

The basic question is... do you enjoy being erotically spanked by your husband? Explore that first and become comfortable with it as an activity, before deciding whether or not you want to tie it into your good or bad behavior. Though if you do, I advise to do it for good behavior. And as I say again and again, only about 30% of what you try works for any one couple, so this may not be for you.

So the final answer for us is that we do the Captain and First Officer thing, and quite infrequent, consensual, erotic spankings on Date Nights when the girls are out of the house. Jennifer doesn't like pain, so on a one to ten scale of intensity, our Date Night "ass-whoopings" score about a two, maybe a three.

Jennifer: Taken in Hand vs. Captain and First Officer...I like our way better.

88 - Don't Wait

May 19, 2011

The last time mum and dad visited us in Connecticut, we had a trip down to the indoor kart track in Wallingford. It's a nice facility and we shelled out the cash, sat through the inane driver instruction video and got started.

Tight track, winding through tires piled five high. The first race dad just edged me out by a tenth of a second. Fair enough and only to be expected, he's the one that has actually done motorsport from well before I was a baby, so he's Ayrton Senna as far as I'm concerned.

The second race he got quicker taking another two-tenths off his lap time. But I was faster still and just nipped him for the win by a tenth of a second. I do remember he had a visible reaction to the lap times like he'd been given a nasty set of labwork results. When you do International Masters karting and your kid that doesn't even have a kart beats you, it's unpleasant.

I don't really remember what I said to him then, but I do remember I was rude.

Last August we visited New Zealand to say goodbye to dad. He was well enough to chat with and hang out, but too sick to leave the house.

Except for the visit to the track.

Dad has been a long time motorsports guy and has done most forms of motorsport over the years... well until I came along and started eating into the budget anyway. But the last form he did was karting and he kept doing that until he was 62 and the cancer started getting a bit much.

But he'd hatched this really stupidly impossible idea to build a full international level kart track in Rotorua. Which naturally means there is now a 90% complete full international level kart track in Rotorua. There's a few bells and whistles around the track to be completed, but the millions of dollars got raised and the track itself is all set.

Dad is a low key guy but very proud of what he'd built, so he came out to play show and tell. Karts are vicious on roads and rip them up quickly, so the track surface is essentially the same material as used on the banking at Daytona. It's smooth as silk too. There's no padding or suspension in a kart but you feel nothing but a smooth ride even at 60+mph.

Naturally I had to have a go. Dad was too sick of course, so he just watched from the pits. I had vaguely planned to do some sort of slowdown and salute move on the front straight as I went past on like the 3rd or 4th lap, but the track is so utterly brilliant that I just couldn't stop pushing it. 100cc karts are not toys and there is moderate danger involved, so your mind tends to become hyper-focused once at race speed. Fastest lap of the day, but nothing amazing due to the wet surface.

Anyway... dad took another four months to die after we left, and that's why the book was five months late. We had actually cashed out my lame 401k in July last year to clear away credit card debt and have a stockpile for spending on the book... but mostly all eaten up with a non-cheap trip to New Zealand to see dad. Then the winter kicked our ass with heating costs. So that's why there was no money for a fancy cover or website design.

Anyway...

I wish he could have read it. I also wish I wasn't rude, about a lot of things.

Don't wait.

89 - How To Purposely Fall Out Of Love As Quickly As Possible

May 28, 2011

When you experience an attraction to another person, your body is dumping dopamine into your system and you experience that dopamine as romantic love. Emotions are not abstract metaphysical experiences, they always have a material world element inside your body. In all seriousness, *emotions are physical things.*

If you're experiencing that emotion for someone who is your spouse and they experience something similar for you back, then it's a pleasant and positive experience for you both. Assuming the relationship is functional, productive and happy, it's quite logical to allow the emotions to continue and encourage them.

However if these emotions develop inside you for someone outside the relationship, things can quickly escalate toward dramatic outcomes. Dopamine is the primary hormone related to pleasure and behavioral motivation and is heavily linked to a Time Before Writing set of programming for mate replacement/opportunistic sex seeking. It's a completely normal biological function and makes perfect sense in the Time Before Writing scenario.

However we aren't in the Time Before Writing anymore, so the biological programming can direct us to seek a mate replacement for a perfectly functional mate in a way that is going to be illogical on a purely rational level. Your body does not understand Marriage 2.0, alimony, child support, restraining orders, not seeing your kids as much, the way having to sell your house in a down market is going to eat equity up and so on. All your body cares about is trying to get a pregnancy started.

So you can have an entire set of emotions devoted to feeling like this new person is your soulmate and you should dump your current spouse, and have another set of quite rational thoughts that doing so would be a colossal effort and cruel to your current spouse. So what to do to get rid of these emotions?

Some easy steps to do as a mindful meditation...by which I mean shoving the Rationalization Hamster in reverse.

Start doing a mentally uncomplicated, but demanding physical activity. For me the ideal task is mowing the lawn. I don't really have to consciously think about mowing the lawn at all, I just run the same pattern every time I do it, but it's also hard work in that I have to push the lawn mower. So it's occupying the part of my brain dealing with automatic physical functions and somewhat hypnotic, but the more conscious rational part of my brain is free to think about things. Seeing as I'm trying to have the rational part of my brain win a battle against the rest of my body, this makes things easier. Other options are walking, running, rowing machines or whatever.

Start consciously thinking about the practical reality of pursuing the other love interest. Emotional and physical affairs grow and develop as fantasy experiences where the spouse never discovers them, no one gets hurt, nothing bad goes wrong and the sex is beyond amazing. That never happens though. You have to start consciously thinking about exactly how the everyday practical reality will play out. Think about the way your wife will absolutely NOT be cool with you hitting something on the side. Imagine her behind the locked bathroom door for hours just screaming at first and then sobbing brokenly. Then when she comes out of the bathroom, the awkwardness of your trying to comfort her and getting a steely eyed two handed shove out of her way in return.

See the big picture. The kids spooked and trying to cope with mom having a melt down and it being dad's fault. Not living here anymore. The kids figuring it out and internally taking a side, but not saying which side it is when they see you every other week or weekend. Or maybe the whole thing just drags out in counseling for a year or two, but never really being the same as it was again. Friends and family finding out and you getting the cold reception in a few places suddenly. The whole trip through the legal waterslide lined with razorblades.

Question the other woman's character. Let's be serious here, if you're married, her responding to your interest or actively hitting on you is a bit of a judgment lapse on her part. What other lapses in judgment does she make? She ever forget her birth control pills? Always used a condom for hook ups? Isn't going to actively try and split your marriage up to have a shot at having you all to herself? When you try and extract yourself from the relationship is she going to start blackmailing you with threats to expose you to your wife? Or if you made the jump to the other woman, would you discover you've really made a trade... down.

Focus on her least attractive body part or qualities. No woman is perfect and they all have terrible weak points. If you hyper-focus on something that kills your attraction, that can be very helpful. I've gotten myself unstuck on one interest when she bent over in front of me and shirt rode up and her pants rode down... and she had stretch-marks on her ass as a total surprise to me. I'm an ass guy so... ewww. The second one had a terrible habit of not using appropriate capitalization in email. Just so annoying to me and a boner killer, and yeah I know that's a really trivial thing to reject someone on, but I'll be damned if I trade down to that. The third just way too intense and needy as my phone blew up with texts etc.

Cut contact. If there's a way to cut contact, do so. Staying in someone's life is not the best way to get untangled out of their life. In time it may be possible to resume contact, but not until the emotional cleansing is complete.

Know the stats. Only 3% of affairs ever turn into a new marriage. Then those marriages fail at spectacular rates. Just assume that if you actively pursue an affair, over the long term you will very likely not still be with either your wife or the other woman.

Given enough time, this set of techniques will remove your romantic feelings for the other woman from you. The deeper you got into her though, the longer it will take to shake it off. Rinse and repeat.

90 - Sometimes It All Gets To Me

June 1, 2011

I get a lot of reader email. A lot of it is win, but some of it is lose. I'm okay with that. It's life and I'm doing what I can.

A recent email got to me though. She unleashed the dreaded "I love you but I'm not in love with you" speech on him and he knew enough to know that things were bad. He scrambled around the Internet for a bit and eventually found his way here. Within a day or so he's getting up to speed on the Alpha Beta thing and orders the book.

Within two weeks he's getting results and she's starting to respond to him better. It's working.

But she started cheating on him three days after the "I love you but I'm not in love with you" speech anyway.

Eleven years together, double virgin relationship start. I had to be the one to tell him that "I gave him a blowjob and he fingered me while I was naked" was very likely not the entire truth.

I'm sorry if this seems to be all about me, but damn it this shit pisses me off. My stuff seriously works and she couldn't wait for it.

And yes... a Girl's Night Out started all this off. So pardon me if I seem a little jaded about GNOs. (Gleeful Nefarious Ovulation) I was pissed off yesterday and pissed off about it today.

And yes for the record I do trust Jennifer. She works all over the state with weekend and evening appointments. She's got a pretty good alibi for anything she wants to get up to. I don't even think about her doing something. But then she doesn't get all dressed up in her man hunting clothes and go out drinking where the Bad Boys are until 2am either. That would set me off big time.

91 - Why Men Are So Paranoid About Girls Night Out

June 1, 2011

Back in the day when I dating my first serious girlfriend Mary, she and a couple of her girlfriends decided to go to a club. Being a squeaky clean Christian, I'd never been to a proper club, but I knew what it was about. So I ran interference and essentially demanded that I get to go along too. (In retrospect, I think the whole thing was just another Fitness Test!) I straight up told her it was a meat market and if she was going, I needed to come too. I think it was one of the few tests I actually passed with flying colors.

About halfway through the night she semi-apologized and agreed that the whole place was a meat market. Overall we had a good time though and I got to end the night with a pretty fantastic makeout session. She actually complained that she was turned on so much that she was struggling with wanting to have sex but she didn't wear down my last minute resistance...

...oh snap. I could have...

Hmmmm... well we didn't have condoms. Imagine how different my life would have been if I got her pregnant that night. Seeing how I was like the damn Baby Sniper with getting Jennifer pregnant... One Shot, One Hospital Bill... it might have played out like that. Oh well... live and yearn.

But anyway....

All that was just innate mate guarding behavior and it's built into every male. Your chosen female is heading into an arena where opportunistic sex with another male may happen with a much better than average likelihood, so you get sick to your stomach and have to do something. Or do nothing and get really sick to your stomach.

Back then I knew nothing of evolutionary psychology, I was just utterly compelled to go run interference and cockblock anyone else interested in her. That was just boyfriend and girlfriend. The stakes with husband and wife are much higher for the man.

Five minutes of a wife being disloyal, can result in 18 years of court mandated support for a child that isn't biologically the husband's. That's about a $100,000 - $200,000 value. If he doesn't, or can't pay the child support for whatever reason (like a job loss), he *will* go to jail. Considering 10% of all children born have mis-identified fathers this is a non-trivial concern and gives most men the absolute heebie-jeebies once they learn of it. If a wife wants to dress up to pull male attention and be at a bar until 2am, a husband that doesn't struggle emotionally with the situation just doesn't understand the extreme jeopardy he is placed in.

But in all seriousness, most men can't even coherently think about the family court system when she's off at the meat market and he's been shamed into staying home. They just have a terrible sinking feeling in the center of the pit of their stomach and psychic dread that the worst thing in the world might be happening built right into them on a biological level.

That's why they go crazy trying to call you.

Their Body Agenda will just assume that their female that purposely abandons them to be proximal to other males in potential mating situations, is up to no good.

And they would be right.

92 - Forgive And Move On Together

June 4, 2011

You're going to get hurt in your marriage. Repeatedly. Welcome to reality.

I'm not just talking about just sex here, though obviously being cheated on ranks right up there at the top of what hurts the most. I'm just saying that your spouse is going to do things to you either out of ignorance, carelessness, revenge or malice that will hurt you. You will find yourself looking at them and wondering what on earth you were thinking when you decided to join your life to theirs.

Jennifer and I have always had a good marriage together and we've strengthened and grown together over time. We're better together now than we have ever been. But that path upwards isn't like riding an escalator, it's a lot of average days, some great days and some truly terrible days. Overall though it's a positive progression. But those truly terrible days can become stumbling blocks to that positive progression if you hold onto them.

Both Jennifer and I have hurt each other badly during our marriage. Almost always these have been unintentional things, but emotional knife blows hurt whether intentional or not. I can think of three events that have made us think that divorce was an option that was about to be placed on the table. One I did to her, one she did to me, and the third was a mutual miscommunication of epic proportions.

I'm not going to explain what those three critical incidents are beyond saying that none of them are related to a third person gaining traction on either one of us. This is just Athol and Jennifer screwing things up with each other big time.

But what we do well as a couple, is forgive one another. We don't hold onto things and repeatedly throw them in each other's faces. When we've made a mess of things with the other, we apologize and try and put things right as best we can. That's right, fucking apologize when you fuck shit up. Your Alpha frame be damned if you just burned your Beta one to the ground. Apologize and put right what you can. Rebuild the comfort you just ruined.

But you can't drag a half-dozen critical incidents through your marriage like pet rocks. They will just weigh you both down and neither one of you will be as happy as you could be. You won't get that positive progression upward together if every time something minorly bad happens you start hurling your pet rocks at your spouse. "Oh yeah? Well what about the time you forgot to pick me up at the airport!" WHAM! "You don't talk to me about anything before you do it! This is exactly the same thing as the time you quit your job without even talking about it first!" WHAM!

So your choice is either to forgive the other and be happier together, or stay mad and keep stoning each other. The trouble is forgiveness is extremely difficult to do... especially when the other person was a total ass and deserves punishment. But it is vastly easier to forgive when the other person apologizes and takes action to start putting things right.

In the end, you need to see each other as being on the same team, rather than on opposing ones. Some days you will win, some days you will lose. But you win and lose as a team.

And be very, very cautious about using the word "divorce" in any argument. Doing so is a critical incident in and of itself.

93 - How To Build Self-Esteem

June 5, 2011

Get a piece of paper and write out what you would do if you had good self-esteem.

Then just start doing the things on the list.

94 - It's Big, It's White And She Can't Wait To Get Her Hands On It

July 16, 2011

Our fridge was starting to die on us yesterday. The giveaway being when eldest daughter went to get some crushed ice and got a whoosh of fairly cool...ish water splurting out over her. I gave it a very hopeful vacuuming out of the air intake as it did look like it had tried to suck several cats up into it. Then we set it on maximum cold and went to bed.

The fridge passed away in the night.

Jennifer snuck out at the crack of dawn to completely avoid the situation by going to work for twelve hours, leaving me, the kids and a dead fridge. Also the cats were out of cat treats and they became increasingly vocal anytime anyone walked into the kitchen. Which seeing we had a dead fridge, was about every seventeen seconds.

So being a smart guy, I pulled the model number and Googled it to find out what the potential problem and part issue/solution was. I'm not a gearhead by any means, but I am a geek and if you can give me a bug sheet and a solution option, I can give it a solid try.

I drove over the lawnmower with the car last year and fixed it with a $20 part including shipping. I did have to toss the entire lawnmower a few weeks ago as I went over something nasty and there was huge "KA-KUNK!" and the engine just burst into tears on me. Then when I pulled on the starting cord, the engine does nothing at all and the wheel the cord pulls on just spins really fast and aimlessly. So I knew I couldn't fix that and just got a new one. One of those top of the line exercise mowers designed to give you a cardio workout as you mow the lawn.

Anyway, I digress. My initial Googling for parts and problems on my fridge model number reveals a somewhat concerning issue with my fridge. Sometimes the compressor breaks and the entire fridge bursts into flame at some random point after that. I figure that I'm not going to mess with that. Better just get a new one.

Anyway, fridge prices vary from "Grrr!" to "Ugh!!" to "WTF!?!" and "We're so sorry for your loss." I'm looking to shop somewhere between Grrr! and Ugh!! Via text I confer with Jennifer about the dilemma and seeing a fridge is a major kitchen appliance that we will live with forever, I figure she wants input. But she's at work and we need a fridge like right now. I simply cannot drink anymore ice cream. Seriously we need to fix this like now.

Honestly we have the cash to get a fridge, but I'd like to spend WTF!?! on upgrading the website and the fridge is eating into that. We don't need a WTF!?! fridge, but an Ugh!! would be nice, and really all we want to spend is Grrr! We text back and forth and settle on fixing the immediate problem with buying a Grrr! fridge thinking that eventually we turn that into the second fridge in the basement for overflow and party planning.

Eldest stays home with the yowling cats and youngest comes fridge shopping with me. As we walk in we pass a cute little grill and it's only a little tickle expensive. Nice. We walk on into the store and I have to say we stumbled onto the perfect sale. We got an Ugh!! fridge on sale for a Grrr! price. I pull up the model number on my phone and Google and the reviews are good. Hot damn. I don't bother asking Jennifer more because I know she will love it. Ugh!! for Grrr! That's name brand Ugh!! to boot. It arrives Wednesday in a four hour window of delivery.

So anyway I'm pumped and gleefully spill the beans to Jennifer who thinks she's getting a Grrr! fridge and a cranky husband. She's excited and I send her photos of daddy's little minions gleefully ransacking the dead fridge of everything into the curbside trash bin that I hauled up into the kitchen. It's fun in the same way demolition is fun. The cats keep complaining about the lack of treats.

Then we have to make a quick trip to get ice and set up a cooler with milk etc for the next few days. Grab a chicken and a little beer. Completely forget to buy cat treats. The cats discuss forming a union.

Jennifer comes home and we retell the day and hunt up the new fridge online for her to just accept what I bought...um I mean see and admire. It's better than the old one, so high marks for getting Ugh!! for Grrr! and handling it all in high spirits. I've roasted a chicken to clear out the outside trash can smell and it's yummy.

After dinner Jennifer and I leave the kids home and do our usual walking circuit where I recount how occasionally the old fridge has that issue where it sometimes bursts into flame. She looks at me funny. So I quickly recover and tell her that I saw that little cute grill. Seeing we did so well on the fridge, we could spring for the grill too. She's agrees. We stop off mid route and buy cat treats before they go all Planet of the Cats on us.

So back to the store with Jennifer and youngest and we spring for the little cute grill. Using Upper Body Strength (TM) I lightly toss the grill into the car and back home we go. I didn't wake up planning to spend that much money. I could have been a grump about it, but all handled and good. Yay me. Jennifer loving it too. We drive back home in good spirits and having fun with each other. Eldest daughter welcomes us home with a pleasant, "Dad there's something funny with the TV..."

Fabulous, just fabulous. What else can happen today?

Oh yeah...

Lemme go unplug the old fridge designed by terrorists.

95 - Functional, Productive and Happy

July 26, 2011

It probably sounds dull, but on the heels of the replacement fridge, (Athol +1) I finally got around to putting in a new faucet for the kitchen sink. The damn thing had been dripping for ages unless you jiggled the handle just right, and it was progressively taking more jiggling. The kids never got the knack and I'd come into the kitchen and find a slow but steady stream of water flowing. It would kinda piss me off, but I never made an issue of it because it just really needed replacing.

Doing anything plumbing related comes with the terror that you will somehow screw it up and many things that should stay dry will get very, very wet in a very short space of time. As it was, it went pretty smoothly and I feel silly for having waited so long. (Athol +1)

I also put together the little grill we collected last weekend. (Athol +1)

My car had an interesting problem on Friday in that I drove out to the goodbye bash for one of my work friends and I couldn't shut the car off and get the key out of the ignition. So I had to turn around and drive to the garage to get that sorted out. Jennifer called ahead and drove out to get me. (Jennifer +1)

That however meant the weekend without my car and I did some driving back and forth getting Jennifer set for her work over the weekend, including some minor lugging of heavy bits and pieces into the van and generally suggesting that I didn't mind being put out a little bit, to save her from being put out a lot. (Athol +1) The weekend was 100 degrees and Jennifer was outside most of the afternoon into the evening and was drenched in sweat when I picked her up at the end of the day. Her reaction to a can of icy cold Cherry Coke awaiting her in the car was bordering on "emotional." (Athol +2)

The exercise routine continues for both of us and we are at the 31 day mark of the Supreme 90 Day DVDs. In all honesty, I'm 41 and she's 38. I believe we took 36 days to get to the 31 day mark. We both push hard when we work out, but we'd both rather cheat days and arrive at the end late but uninjured than have to stop. It's an intense program and I'm drenched in sweat like I've never been before.

According to the fancy scale, I've lost 3% body fat since we started... but I've not lost any weight. So minus six pounds of fat, plus six pounds of muscle. I shit you not. I have some ways to go to "buff", but am noticeably better all around with tone and strength. I'm gonna give me a +3 on the work so far.

Jennifer actually has gained a pound since starting. Toned and tighter. Ass = Ass +1. Schwing! She gets major points from me for sticking with it too. It's been really fun doing it together. She does so much for me anyway that she gains points here and there all the time. The sex has been sensational this past month.

Been listening to the Lord of the Rings soundtrack in the car today and had a mild twinge of homesickness. As we walked the final leg of our circuit home today, it spilled over into a 15-20 second altered state where the extreme weirdness of living in a place 10,000 miles from New Zealand felt like free falling in emotional zero-G. How did I get here?! Looking at Jennifer happily pacing beside me and a quarter step behind sparking the same sensation... how did I find you?!

It's nice to think that perhaps we were meant to find each other to serve some purpose. It would be as Gandalf says, "An encouraging thought." More likely though, the dopamine is just running high and I'm feeling particularly in love with her today.

She is my home.

<u>96 - Shit My Husband Says: Ocean Voyage</u>

July 29, 2011

Jennifer writes this post.

I'm exhausted to the point of falling asleep on the couch and gently prodded awake by Athol after sleeping for who knows how long. I edit the night's post as best my sleepy brain can and we head off to bed...

Athol: You look beat, you want to skip?

Jennifer: No, we can do something.

Athol: You're on the bottom, sleepy baby.

Jennifer: Yes! (I love being on the bottom)

Athol: You don't look like you want to orgasm though.

Jennifer: No, not really. Tired.

Athol: So what would you like? Gentle Jostle, Ocean Voyage, or Almost Raping?

Jennifer: Hahaha...the first and last I get, but what's Ocean Voyage?

He doesn't actually answer me, just climbs on top of me and with the duvet still between us sets a steady rolling rhythm while kissing my neck. Don't ask me how he thinks this stuff up on the fly, but he does it all the time.

Jennifer: Okay, Ocean Voyage. You're incorrigible.

Athol: The weather might get a little rough toward the end.

Jennifer: Hahaha

Athol: On your stomach or back. Just decide.

True confession. I'm happy to get him off, but I'm also tired and it will finish much faster on my stomach. I stretch out face down and he pulls the duvet clear off the bed and climbs on top of me.

We have a short and sweet "Ocean Voyage."

Athol: Thank you for your compliance.

Jennifer: Thank you for your consideration.

Athol: I'm just happy that you think being held face down and fucked is me being considerate.

Good grief he's an ass lol.

Yep...that's my life. Not a bad deal and I like that he keeps me laughing.

97 - The Main Complaint About Monogamy Is That It Works

August 10, 2011

I got a long reader email that has far too many identifying marks to edit, so the short version is he is trying to decide whether or not to marry his girlfriend of 2.5 years. By his account she is wife material and a good match for him. Her sex drive seems higher than his, but the main stumbling point is he's cheated on her 3-4 times and gotten away with it already, and just can't get past the idea of getting married and not getting a little something on the side once in a while. After all, per evolutionary psychology, that's how men are wired. Right?

Athol: There's not a perfect solution to choose.

You are correct that monogamy isn't natural and that men and women are biologically wired to have a primary partner and opportunistic sex with others. However much of our modern society isn't natural. Democracy isn't natural, nor is capitalism, or education, the rule of law, hospitals, flushing toilets and plentiful food. (Autotuned pop music isn't natural either, so that I guess slightly ruins the point I'm making because let's face it, autotune is awful.)

Or put another way, it's perfectly natural for bigger guys to pound skinny guys into the sand and just take their women from them. If you want the real stats, over the course of human history only about 40% of males ever get to make a female pregnant. All perfectly natural. Monogamy is a social construct that benefits all men except the most attractive ones (who no longer get multiple women). Most men whining about monogamy being a curse and a shackle actually do much better sexually in a monogamous culture than a non-monogamous one. The "average guy" complaint is essentially that monogamy actually gets the "average guy" a sexual partner instead of being pounded into the sand, or just watching the woman he loves shun him for being average.

So if you want to marry her, I think you just have to bite the bullet and understand that by marrying her you are making a choice that has positives and negatives. You get a faithful, permanent partner and an ideal situation for raising children. The cost is opportunistic sex.

If you don't want to marry her, that's fine, but you should come to that decision quickly to allow her to find a man that wants marriage and children (assuming she wants that).

But as you realize, if you continue cheating on her, eventually you will be caught and then you are in a far worse situation than you would be if you never married her.

Something else to consider is that after banging your girlfriend for 2.5 years, if she hasn't gotten pregnant, as far as your Body Agenda is concerned, she's infertile and a poor choice of mate so you will find yourself mentally driven to find ways to get sex with others. No doubt birth control is involved, but try explaining that to your body.

Another thing to think about is that the desire for outside sex doesn't seem to ever go away. I still experience that myself at 41, though my sex drive is much higher than yours. Mostly it doesn't bother me, some days it does. Also it's absolutely nothing to do with Jennifer who is a willing and good partner sexually. I've tried getting her to wear a red wig, but Jennifer's Australian accent is appallingly bad and just ruins the fantasy of banging Nicole Kidman. So there doesn't seem to be a perfect solution to management of that desire for a little something on the side.

Also if she wants sex four times a week and you only twice, over the long term that can become more of a problem in that you may not ultimately be able to satisfy her sexually. Her drive can continue to tick up into her 30's and yours can wind down a little in your 40's.

So in the end, there is no perfect solution to all this. You just have to make a choice and live with it.

(Yeah yeah I know I'm showing my age with a Nicole Kidman reference. Bite me. I also watch "Wizards of Waverly Place" because I think the mom character is hot. This is in no way awkward.)

98 - The Best Pussy I Ever Had

August 20, 2011

Max is the best cat I've ever had.

I found him as a tiny kitten utterly lost, crying and stumbling across the back lawn one Saturday. A scrap of black fur inconveniently placed in front of my mower. We bottle fed him for a while and he pulled through just fine. The girls were so little then, everyone got their ba-bas, and no doubt Max thinks he's one of our kids. He's also calm and affectionate with visiting kids and toddlers and always quietly leads them on the guided tour of the house, ending in the kitchen and him staring at the drawer with the cat treats.

Max is exceptionally smart, knowing everyone's pattern of movements and sleeping schedules. During the week, he will climb on Jennifer in bed by 7:00am to make sure she's up. On the weekend, Max sleeps in too. On Jennifer's work from home days he sits on the chair next to her and naps on and off, with periodic prompts for strokes and cuddles. He greets everyone as they come in the house as a sort of feline doorman. Artful Dodger style, he will hit up both girls and Jennifer in turn and fleece all three of them into giving him cat treats within a half hour span. I figure he gets enough treats, plus I don't want to be nagged for treats all day, so I pass on treat giving for the most part. I'd see him staring at the cat treat drawer in the kitchen and I'd just pretend I didn't see him.

As a result, Max started using a system of asking to go out the back door and then immediately asking to come back in, and then gave me that "Oh while you're up and I have your attention..." look and would walk to the cat treat drawer and stare at it. He got me a few times with this I admit.

Being behavior minded, I fixed him of his "outside-inside-get me treats" plan by letting him out the backdoor and then simply walking away for 10-15 minutes before letting him back in. If he wants out, he can go out. If he wants treats, it's an annoying waste of time for him. I also only give Max treats once a day - usually when he is not asking for them - and then ignore his requests for more treats. As a result he doesn't keep bugging me for treats. But he does bug everyone else because they just go "awwww Maxy-Waxy wantz moar num-nums" and pile them in front of him like Cleopatra buying off Julius Caesar.

Using a method known as "lightly tossing", Max has learned to not climb over me in bed. Everyone else wakes up with a chance of sharing a bed with Max. He's a...ah... close sleeper and puts his head on your pillow about a third of the time. So sorry Max, but the facesitting position has been filled.

His other name is "Inconvenient Placement Cat." The family catch phrase being "Inconvenient Placement Cat is placed inconveniently." Max has learned that he can sprawl in a high traffic area and everyone will step over him and he's quite safe to do so. The middle of the hall. On the stairs. Doorways. Anywhere you want to put your feet, there he is lying blissfully semi-conscious. Unless you want to pick up him and move him, people are formally required to perform a clog dance to get him to move, which is quite difficult when one is moving a sofa.

However after several quite accidental cat punting episodes, Max has learned that black cats should not be placed inconveniently in dark rooms at night when I'm not wearing my glasses. The eight foot path between my side of the bed and the bathroom being notable for said punting episodes. I always feel bad after these events and check and cuddle him and the last couple times I swear he looked at me to say, "No actually that was totally my fault for sleeping there. Don't beat yourself up about it. But if it would make you feel better, maybe we could get through this awkward moment if you gave me some treats."

Max is getting older so we don't play rough together quite so much now. It usually starts as a game of me playfully pinning his tail or back legs and just holding them. Flap-flap-flap-flap-flap goes Max's tail on the floor giving me the warning that he'll play rough if I want to play rough, but there's no crying. At some point it's all on and he moves unbelievably fast and pounces on my hand and arm. I seriously have no hope of avoiding him. He's all muscle, claws and teeth and it's both scary and amazing to watch him. I have a couple of minor scars from him, but if he really wanted to hurt me I'd have stopped messing with him long ago. I just view it as all my fault for messing with him and get through the awkward moment by having some ice cream as a treat.

If Max doesn't want to play rough, he just gets up, walks away and ignores me in favor of Jennifer or the girls. Which is exactly what I do to him, about the behavior I don't want to see of his.

He's a very quiet cat too. He just wanders around calmly and does what he wants to do. It's like he's reserved meowing for emergencies or something. If he does meow at all loudly, the entire family snaps to instant attention and checks on Max.

You can love him and cuddle him for hours on end and he'll soak it all in. On the days Jennifer and the girls are all out somewhere and I'm home alone for most of the day, I break my one treat policy and give him treats three or four times. He's a good cat, being good, so he can have treats.

I'd tell you about our other cat, but he's as dumb as mud. He looks at the cat door like it's a freaking Rubik's Cube.

(Behavior management works on people and animals equally well. Words don't matter, actions do. Reward the behavior you want to continue, ignore the behavior you don't. As long as you

have something they need that they can't otherwise get, you're in charge.)

99 - Sexting and Jennifer's Lost Phone

August 22, 2011

A while back I mentioned that I have a lot of my most frequent phone contacts listed in my phone with a numbering system. That way they stay at the top of my contact list for easy access. The current set up is:

1 Jennifer
2 Safety
3 Eldest Daughter
4 Youngest Daughter
5 and below are work contacts...

"2 Safety" is actually my own phone number, that way if I somehow miss key a dirty message to Jennifer, I might slip one number down, but not two. All that happens is I text myself a dirty message. It's texturbation.

Now Jennifer has a very similar numbering system for her phone too. But once in a while I grab her phone when she's in the shower or something, and quickly change my name in her contacts list to something a little more edgy than merely "1 Athol." Something like...

Big Daddy
Happy Penis Man
1-800-HUSBAND
1-900-HOTSTUD
It's Business Time
The Captain

So when I call her, my name pops up on her caller ID as "Spanking Tonight" or something else hopefully panty melting using my patented "Goofy and Groping" style of Game. Usually it just cracks her up and sometimes embarrasses her a little if it pops up at an inopportune time. So I usually unleash the first contact while she's driving to work in the morning. Then I figure she can change the name back in her contact list, or she just wants to be getting calls from "MILF Casting Agent" at risky moments.

Then she lost her phone...

Somewhere at a fair she lost her phone with one of my stupid names still on it. Somehow I just know this is going to come around and bite me in the ass. We're looking all over place for the phone and just not finding it, so eventually I just have to break down and start calling her phone, hoping someone with both a sense of humor and decency will have picked up the phone.

It took six calls before this guy answers Jennifer's phone.

He sounded very... uncomfortable.

After a short conversation I explained my wife had lost her phone and I was calling it to try and track it down. As fortune had it, he lived about two miles away and I said I'd come over and pick it up. It's her phone, she lost it, but apparently my stupid name trumps that and I'm now the responsible party. So I drive over there and ring the front door bell. This middle-aged guy comes to the door and before I can say "Hi I'm here for my wife's phone." he holds up the phone and with this sour, tired look on his face says to me.

"Are you... Cockzilla?"

Of course I have to identify myself as Cockzilla because I want the damn phone back.

"I am."

Now as he hands me the phone like it's contaminated, around the corner of his living room, comes a woman who I guess was his mother because she looks 75 years old... going on dead. She's riding one of those little Rambler electric wheelchairs and hooked up to oxygen, with a cigarette in one hand. There's like two inches of ash hanging off the end of this cigarette as well. She's the Queen of the land of Emphysema. Then with this horrible raspy voice she says...

"I'm going to need to see some ID."

100 - Due Diligence Before You Marry

August 23, 2011

When you rent an apartment, all the landlord truly cares about is, (1) will you be able to pay the rent, (2) are you going to trash the apartment, and (3) are you going to turn the dining room into a meth-lab. So if the landlord has even a walnut sized brain, before they lease the apartment to you, they run credit and criminal background checks on you. If all checks out, you get the apartment.

The landlord does not care if you are pretty.

When you meet a woman and start thinking about moving from a non-serious relationship into a serious one, all you tend to automatically care about is whether or not she is pretty.

If you don't check her out fully and are lucky, she also happens to be able to (1) hold a job, (2) help keep the house clean, and (3) is fairly healthy. Enjoy the sweet beauty of true love and romance.

But if you didn't check her out fully and are unlucky, she (1) has some sort of serious money and/or employment issue, (2) is only slightly more housebroken than a flock of geese, and (3) has some sort of major health or addiction issue. Which means you're screwed.

As an example of one of those "little surprises" that one learns about after the wedding, Jennifer had $17,000 in student loans that I had no clue about. After the initial shock I moved on fairly quickly as I got to understand the American college expenses better and it's not like Jennifer was living some kind of lavish party girl lifestyle at college. Plus by this time I was married already, so it's past the point of no return to decide whether or not $17,000 was going to be a deal breaker in marrying her anyway. It's not like two months into the marriage I could suddenly take the moral high ground and say "You withheld need to know information from me" and high tail it back to New Zealand. Especially not after I had just fled New Zealand to avoid paying my student loan.

So while I do believe romantic love is a wonderful thing and an important part of a happy marriage, it isn't enough by itself to have a happy marriage. The purpose of marriage is to have a functional, productive and happy life together. So in order to do that, you need to marry a functional, productive and happy person. Plus you need to be one yourself.

At the very least you should do some basic due diligence and find out about your partners credit, criminal and health histories before you sign on the dotted line and legally bind yourself to them.

Wikipedia - *"Due diligence" is a term used for a number of concepts involving either an investigation of a business or person prior to signing a contract, or an act with a certain standard of care. It can be a legal obligation, but the term will more commonly apply to voluntary investigations. A common example of due diligence in various industries is the process through which a potential acquirer evaluates a target company or its assets for acquisition.*

If nothing else, sneak a look in her damn medicine cabinet and see if she has a little city of Batshit Crazy meds in there.

(As an aside my parents paid off my small student loan as a post wedding gift. I did intend to pay it, um... eventually, but Mum and Dad worried that I might get myself into a tax/late

payment nightmare before I managed to pay it off. They were probably right. I would also like to apologize to the people of New Zealand for taking an entire educational investment in myself and immediately moving to another country as soon as it was finished. It's not you New Zealand, you're just great, it's me.)

101 - The Sci-fi Thing And Just Being Yourself

October 4, 2011

Some comments from yesterday's post – "Girl Game: When You're Too Low Maintenance… Add A Touch of Klingon."

Anonymous said... Athol, honest question, why all the sci-fi? Is it personal preference, you think it gets the message over more effectively that anything else or that the people you're trying to reach are often geeks and would understand the idiom?

Looking Glass said... Two thoughts on the sci-fi:

1) Athol's a nerd, never forget that.
2) The point of Sci-Fi is abstraction, allowing for a discussion of the present from a foreign point of view. Which is a lot of what Athol's work is.

Athol: The short answer is yes to everything. The longer answer is that I'm just being myself.

Yes I do like sci-fi. I've read and watched a ton of it and it's just in my veins so to speak. Jennifer likes sci-fi too, so that's a big win as well. There's been plenty of times in my life where I've found myself talking to a very attractive woman and been quite drawn to her, and then she reveals some sort of basic confusion between Star Wars and Star Trek and my erection just ebbs away never to return. Seriously, Captain Picard does NOT become Darth Vader, does that really have to be explained to anyone? I must do something with my face as well when they unload their ignorance on me, as I've seen the look cross their face of, "Oh that was the wrong thing to say to this guy for some reason."

So I draw from what I know. That's how stuff ends up in posts. I have no idea how some of it turns up, it just does. I get that Jimmy Neutron brain blast thing happening sometimes.

Yes I do think some of it is better taught from the sci-fi angle. The main thing I do this with is the Captain and First Officer metaphor for a husband and wife dynamic. It is enormously difficult to explain any form of male leadership or dominance without getting immediately screamed at as some kind of wife beating bigot. Everyone immediately goes on the defensive and is concerned that the wife is going to be taken advantage of. Male dominance can so easily be reframed as female subjugation if you aren't careful.

The Captain and First Officer role however is instantly understood by anyone familiar with Star Trek, and quickly understood by those that don't with the follow up explanation of "it's kinda like a pilot and a co-pilot in a commercial airliner." The trick is both the Captain role and the First Officer role, are positive and strong/meaningful roles in a relationship. It's also a little goofy to use Star Trek as a marriage advice source. As a result, no one gets defensive about listening to the concept. Women that would be extremely angry at the suggestion they deep down want a male lead relationship or being submissive, often immediately explode with an "OMG that's exactly how I feel!!! I want to be a First Officer!!!"

For some women it's a total mindfuck to realize they've gotten two decades into a marriage actively working hard to avoid getting what they really want from the relationship.

And yes, I'm trying to reach geeks. Let's face it, the beautiful people of the world don't need help getting laid, and there's only a tiny minority of them. The rest of us can learn ways to improve ourselves and there's a great mass of us. At the end of the day I'm trying to make a living at this too and it's simple do-the-math-thinking.

But beyond all that, I really just don't care too much what anyone thinks anymore. I'm very much *out* as a person these days. I'm out about my sexual interests. I'm out about my thoughts. I'm out about being an atheist. I'm out about sci-fi. I'm out about what I eat for dinner some nights lol.

So there are lots of reasons someone could decide to dislike me, or not like something about me. But there are also a lot of reasons someone could decide to like me, or like something about me. So either way, there's opportunity for a strong reaction one way or the other. The people that don't like me leave a pissy comment and then move on. The people that don't care either way move on too. But people that like me stick around and if they keep liking me they become fans, and fans buy books and tell their friends about the blog and book.

When people say "Just be yourself", what they really mean is "Don't nerf your personality into the ground trying to be someone that no one could actively dislike." Because if you do that, you're taking away everything about you that someone could like about you too.

When you are yourself, you tend to attract people to you that are also into the same things as you. If you love hiking, tell people you love hiking, ask women to go hiking with you, join a hiking club, actually hike somewhere. At some point someone will probably say, "Oh you should meet Tina, she likes hiking too", and then you go game Tina. Don't game someone into being your girlfriend and then discover she hates hiking. Then especially don't complain that she's Fitness Testing you about your hiking. Or maybe you just stop hiking altogether to keep the peace. See how that works?

Jennifer loves sci-fi too. When I first met her, Star Trek: Deep Space Nine piloted and we watched it together in a group in one of her friend's dorm room. We don't watch that much TV, but we've watched Deep Space Nine, Voyager, Babylon 5, Battlestar Galactica and Stargate SG-1 together cozyed up on the sofa together. We're hopeful about Terra Nova so far. So that's something that's worked for us. So when I texted her earlier today...

Athol: "*Imzadi...* do you think I use too many sci-fi references on the blog?"

Jennifer: "LMAO."

See... you may not get that, *but she gets it*. She gets me. And that's all that matters.

Further Resources

Married Man Sex Life
www.marriedmansexlife.com

Athol writes nearly daily posts at the blog. If you liked this book, you'll like the blog, mostly because Athol just shamelessly slapped a bunch of posts together to make this book.

The Married Man Sex Life Primer 2011

The Primer is Athol's flagship book, and will be updated annually with his latest thoughts and improvements. It contains a vast array of information and practical approaches to improving your marriage and sex life. The 2011 edition runs 344 pages and is available in print and Kindle on Amazon, and as a PDF on Lulu. Links to all three editions are on the blog.

The Primer is intended to be updated annually. The 2012 edition is aimed at a March 2012 release.

Coming Soon

In no particular order: More books, coaching, seminars, DVDs, books on tape and anything else Athol can convince you to buy to support his dreams of world domination.

About the Author and his Wife

Athol Kay is an innovative thinker, humorist and family man with a one track mind.

He is a "Mixed Marital Artist" combining a variety of relationship approaches from evolutionary psychology, Pickup Artist "Game", sociology, biology, life experience, romance novels, crappy women's magazines, far too many books, blogging, behavior modification and cheap porn. He has distilled all this research into a few outstandingly effective tactics for gaining happiness and sex in marriage.

Jennifer Kay is the author's wife and she is mentioned 244 times in this book. She edits and approves all of Athol's writing before he publishes it. This is in no small part due to his lack of grammar, but mainly because Athol occasionally says things about her that her mother might read.

Athol was born in New Zealand and met Jennifer nine days before he was due to fly home after working on a summer camp in Maryland in 1991. Long distance for three years, they finally married in 1994. Married for 17 years, they have two daughters and live in Connecticut. They have a carefully balanced relationship where Athol dreams up all kinds of weird stuff, and Jennifer doesn't leave him.

Made in the USA
Lexington, KY
23 March 2013